EXPLORING ELIZABETHAN

BY DOROTHY CLARKE

WITH DESIGNS BY STEPHANIE POWELL

Embroidery threads used throughout this book were supplied by Warnaar Trading Company Limited.
The Linen used in most of the items in this book was supplied by Margaret Barrett Distributors Limited.

Published by Georgeson Publishing Limited
P.O.Box 100-667, North Shore Mail Centre, Auckland, New Zealand.
Phone: 64 9 410 2079 Facsimile: 64 9 410 2069
E mail: gpl@georgeson.co.nz
www.georgeson.co.nz

ISBN 0 473 03634 7

©1997 Georgeson Publishing Limited

First Published February 1997, first reprint March 1997
Second reprint June 1997, third reprint May 1998,
fourth reprint November 1998, fifth reprint May 1999,
sixth reprint December 1999

Series Editor: Pru Georgeson
Photography: Becky Nunes
Layout and Illustrations: Valancy Stevens

Printed in New Zealand

ACKNOWLEDGMENTS

I would like to take this opportunity to thank Betty Logan for introducing me to coloured silk embroidery in the style of the Elizabethan period. Without her introduction I might never have become involved in this most fascinating technique.

There are many others who have helped, encouraged and supported me in many ways. My students, from the many classes I have taught over the years, who told me I must write down my notes, pass on my stitch diagrams and record my tips. My friends and my family, who have always believed in me, particularly my late daughter Jocelyn. I would finally like to thank Josephine Slack and Lynette Hale for their help.

Dorothy Clarke, 1996.

CONTENTS

Coloured silk embroidery of the Elizabethan period is rich in texture, extravagant in its use of colour, generous in the variety of stitches used and lavish in the employment of beads and metal threads. Needlewomen of that period had a wide repertoire of stitches at their 'fingertips' and used a beautiful assortment of threads, some of which are no longer available.

I consider my work to be 'New Elizabethan'. I have not confined myself to reproducing the work of the past, instead I have looked to the past for inspiration, but I have experimented with the fabric and threads available today. I present here Elizabethan embroidery for the modern embroiderer. The range of stitches used by the seventeenth century needlewoman was impressive - here I introduce you to the stitches and techniques they used with clear, easy-to-follow stitch diagrams and instructions. I do hope you will share my pleasure in learning this delightful technique and experience the pleasure I have found in 'my Elizabethan journey'.

Dorothy Clarke, November 1996.

How to use this Book

This book has been written for the embroiderer who would like to learn a new and different technique. Colourful and textured, this is embroidery for embroiderers. Coloured Silk Embroidery of the Elizabethan period was originally used on clothes and furnishings so the threads used to embroider this are slightly heavier than the stranded cottons we are all so used to. You will find they are lovely to use and the resultant texture adds fresh interest to your embroidery. The main stitches used are variations of the buttonhole stitch, not a difficult stitch to master!

This book is set out in sections, the first 'History of the Embroidery' gives some background to the technique and the second 'Necessities' outlines the fabric, threads and needles used in creating this embroidery, plus how to transfer the designs and finishing off techniques.

We then move on to the 'Stitch Section' where we cover the stitches used. We give large, clear, easy-to-follow diagrams with accompanying instructions. With these instructions you will be amazed at how easy it is to learn new stitches!

The next section is the 'Shape Section' This section is pivotal to the rest of the book. Here we give details of the needles, threads and stitches used to embroider *each* of the flowers, leaves, insects and bird found in this book. All the flowers etc used in this book are shown on the Sampler - you may or may not choose to stitch the Sampler, it does not matter. Full instructions for stitching each flower, leaf and insect are given in the shape section and these instructions apply to each shape whether it is stitched on the pin cushion, cat, nymph or an embroidery of your own design.

We give seven full colour pages of the embroidery which features in this book, one page is devoted to each different project to give you the opportunity to use the photographs as a reference when you are doing your own embroidery. The eighth page gives a selection of work embroidered by Dorothy's former pupils.

In the final section of this book we cover the instructions given to create the different projects we show in colour on pages 51 - 57. To highlight the different ways this technique can be used we have included big as well as small, modern as well as very traditional uses of this technique. In some of the projects we have used different colours to those used in the Sampler, for example the pomegranate in the 'Swete Bage'. Where this is done we give the threads used to stitch the pomegranate on the 'Swete Bage' in with the 'Swete Bage' instructions. But for detailed instructions on how to stitch the pomegranate you will need to refer to the instructions for the pomegranate in the shape section.

We have given you some ideas on how to use this delightful technique. On page 58 we show you how Dorothy's former pupils have gone on to use the technique, but don't stop here, the possibilities are endless. For clothing, try the new random dyed threads on a solid background colour, the effect is stunning, or experiment with tone on tone for textured interest. Mirror backs, box lids, chatelaines and bags can all be stitched most attractively in this technique, the only limit is time and your imagination! Experiment and enjoy the challenge of stitching in a technique that was last popular four centuries ago!

HISTORY OF COLOURED SILK EMBROIDERY (1558-1603)

The Elizabethan embroiderer was a most accomplished needlewoman.

In Elizabethan England in the sixteenth century embroidery once again flourished. English embroidery, *opus anglicanum*, had been much sought after by churchmen throughout Europe from the mid-thirteenth century until the end of the fourteenth century. However, by the Elizabethan period embroidery had moved from ecclesiastical, to secular and domestic work, and whilst professional embroiderers were still common, the domestic embroiderer was increasingly skilled.

The sixteenth century was a period of peace and prosperity with increased wealth, particularly in the middle and upper classes and with this there was an associated rise in living standards. Two excellent ways of displaying a family's wealth were by richly decorating their homes and their persons.

Embroidery was used in Tudor households to create a feeling of opulence and warmth. The quantity of decorated upholstery, curtains, and embroidered borders on household linen served as an obvious and very visible indicator of wealth. Whilst vanity in clothing in this period reached heights not seen since. Men's clothing fashions changed even more quickly than women's and they all enjoyed wearing fabrics lavishly adorned with stitchery, gold and precious stones.

Embroidery in this period was aided by the improved quality of the steel needles that became available and also by the arrival of the first pattern books. One of the earliest surviving publications containing designs specifically for embroidery was published in Germany by Johannes Schonsperger (*c.* 1523). By 1550 several pattern books were available, but it was the herbals and bestiaries with their woodcut illustrations which were particularly suited to interpretation by embroiderers that really provided inspiration for the Elizabethan's. Some of the illustrations from these publications still in existence show that the drawings were pricked with pins for pouncing on to the fabric. The illustrations included wild and garden flowers, fruits, animals, birds and insects. There was no attempt to show any relation in actual size between the various objects shown.

Flower gardens became fashionable. The discovery of new countries with new plants and animals which were painted by artists further fostered the developing interest in flowers. These illustrations were used by embroiderers for their designs so that embroidery during the reign of Elizabeth I could almost be said to 'burst into flower'.

Coloured silk embroidery was one of three types of embroidery which were very popular in this period. Blackwork was also popular and can be seen in many portraits from this period. Whitework, consisting of drawn threadwork fillings and reticella motifs reached a peak in its execution by the end of the sixteenth century when court dress dictated a starched, standing ruff, also to be seen in portraits of the period.

The predominant decorative style for coloured silk embroidery was the scrolling stem pattern enclosing flowers. This stem was shaped to create separate areas each filled with garden and country flowers and enriched with a variety of insects and tiny animals to fill all the available space. The colours chosen to embroider the flowers frequently bore no relation to their appearance in nature. Threads used were silk and many forms of metal thread. The embroidery was further enriched by the liberal addition of spangles, beads, pearls and other jewels. These designs appeared on coifs and bodices, tunics, skirts, dresses, hats and gloves. They also appeared on household furnishings such as cushions, bedspreads and long pillows. Numerous stitches were used including a variety of chain and buttonhole stitches, stem, back, satin and long and short stitch, knots, ladder, coral, Ceylon and plaited stitch, plaited braid, Algerian eye, interlacing, long armed cross, two-sided Italian cross and many more. The embroidery was entirely on the surface and the whole effect was very rich, very textural and quite exuberant.

Necessities

Fabrics

The embroidery in this book is heavy and textured and because of this a firm, closely-woven fabric is recommended. We have used Antique White crewel linen from Czechoslovakia which is 100% linen. However, any good quality, closely-woven fabric is suitable for this embroidery. To give the fabric additional strength, needed because all the embroidery is on the surface, we recommend the use of 'Stayflex'. This is a woven, iron-on fabric interlining and should be ironed on to the fabric before starting to stitch.

Threads

The main thread used for the embroidery throughout this book is DMC Coton a broder 16. Coton a broder 16 is thicker than stranded cottons and easier to use as the strands of thread will not separate. Its heavier weight makes it ideal for the stitch techniques shown here. Coton perle No. 8 can also be used as it is the same weight as Coton a broder 16 but it is only available in a smaller range of colours and larger quantities. Today a lot of embroiderers random dye their own threads and these can be used most attractively. Any thread of a similar weight to the coton a broder 16 is suitable for use in this embroidery, just avoid threads that are stranded as they tend to separate and it is harder to achieve a neat finished result.

The use of metallic threads is entirely optional but it is in the tradition of the original Elizabethan work where silver and gold threads were used generously to give added sparkle and lustre to the embroidery.

The range of metallic threads available now gives us a much greater choice than earlier needlewomen had. DMC have a range called Fil metallise that comes in a variety of shades, Madeira have a Metallic range as do Sulky and Gutermann. All these threads, and many more of a similar nature, can be used in the sewing machine as well as in hand embroidery. Where we use these threads we have stitched them in the needle *with the coton a broder* and stitched them as one thread. In the text you will notice we refer to multi-coloured metallic thread or bronze metallic thread, feel free to use whatever you have in your sewing basket, or this could be the right time to buy yourself a selection of these threads.

Where we have used gold or silver metallic thread to further embellish the embroidery we have used Gold DMC thread No. 282 and Silver DMC Fil Argent Clair. Through the instructions for the embroidery it is just referred to as 'gold metallic thread' or 'silver metallic thread' and you can use the threads we have suggested or once again substitute for something similar in your work basket. Where different threads have been used they are mentioned in the instructions on how to stitch each shape.

Needles

This embroidery is worked using No. 8 crewel needles, No. 24 or 26 tapestry needles and No. 10-13 beading needles or No. 10 straw needles. The crewel needle has a long eye and a sharp point and is used to work chain stitch in the ground fabric. The tapestry needle has a long eye but a blunt tip and is used for the majority of the stitching. The beading or straw needles are long and fine and are used to stitch the beads, sequins and rhinestones to the embroidery.

Handy Hints

• Do not unpick threads when a mistake is made. It is better to cut out any mistakes as the thread frays and looses its sheen when unpicked. Always re-start with a new thread.

• When using DMC gold or silver thread I dab the cut end, where the threads have a tendency to separate, on to my UHU glue stick. This does not hurt the embroidery as the work must be washed on completion.

EMBELLISHMENTS

It is important to add 'glitz' to Elizabethan work. Originally precious jewels - pearls, rubies and diamonds were added to the garments. Today sequins, beads and diamantes are added to achieve the same effect.

SCISSORS

There are many different types of scissors available. For this embroidery a blunt-nosed pair which can be used to push dacron inside shapes and snip the odd thread are what is required.

HOOP

This embroidery does not need to be worked in a frame. The chain stitch which is worked around each shape initially must be worked in the hand as the stitches must be very small and they can not be stitched small enough if worked in a frame.

However, if you feel more comfortable holding your embroidery in a frame you will need either a small circular hoop about 10 cms in diameter which can be used to encircle a small area or a hoop large enough to include the entire design. In this instance a rectangular slate frame could be advisable. It is important that the embroidery is not flattened after it is worked when re-positioning the hoop.

Personally I only work the strawberry in a frame, I find the rest can quite comfortably be worked held in your hand.

EXTRAS

There are a number of other items which are also necessary when working this type of embroidery.

• Dacron batting or a soft cushion filling is used to push underneath completed embroidery to give the embroidery a raised appearance.
• Felt, a little of this is cut to the shape of the strawberry fruit, the stitching is then worked over this padding to give a raised appearance to the strawberry.
• Pen, fine tip UNI-ball-Micro-deluxe-waterproof pen, this must be waterproof, it is used for putting the design on your fabric.

To Transfer the Design

Embroiderers frequently ask me which method I find the best for transferring a design to fabric. Personally I prefer to use a light box.

A commercial light-box can be bought or made then the design to be traced is placed on the glass, cover with the fabric and trace the main outlines of the design with the UNI-ball-Micro-deluxe-waterproof pen. The one danger with this technique is that there can be no mistakes in tracing the design. If you prefer you could use a soft lead pencil. Make sure you centre the design on your fabric and *trace only the main outlines* of the design, *do not* transfer any fine details as they will not be hidden by subsequent stitching.

If you do not have a light box there are alternatives, photocopy the design, darken with a black felt tip pen, tape it to your window and then tape the fabric over the top of the design and trace. Whichever method you use do make sure you trace the design onto the centre of the fabric keeping it on the straight of the material. The design can be traced onto your fabric before or after you iron on the stayflex interlining.

Finishing Off or 'Blocking'

This embroidery is not completed until you have embroidered the date of its completion and your name on a corner of the linen. It may last hundreds of years and a date and your name will give it extra value and interest in the years ahead!

This embroidery *must not be ironed* when it is completed. If ironed it will lose the lovely texture you have created with your surface stitchery and padding.

Method

Take the soft pinex board and place the 1 cm grid graph paper on top of the board. Then cover the whole board and graph paper with the waterproof acetate. It is extremely important that the dampness from your embroidery cannot get through to the pinex board as this could stain your embroidery.

Now completely soak your embroidery by gently washing it in a mild soap (Lux or Sunlight) and then stretch it out onto the board placing the top of the material along a line on the graph paper, stretch firmly.

Put tacks along the top of the material at 3 to 4 cm intervals. Now stretch the material down along the left and right hand sides keeping it an equal distance from the nearest line on each side and placing tacks at 3 to 4 cm intervals. Finally tack along the bottom of the embroidery once again placing tacks at 3 to 4 cm intervals.

Your work is now 'blocked' and must be left tacked like this until it is completely dry. Blocking removes any puckers or wrinkles and serves as an alternative to ironing which is not suitable with this technique.

Requirements

- Soft pinex board at least 10 cm bigger than your embroidery - a cake board or ceiling tile works well.
- Graph paper, preferably about a 1 cm grid - the lines on the graph paper are extremely useful when it comes to stretching your embroidery and keeping it square.
- Waterproof acetate, duraseal, or contact.
- Tack pins (for blocking) rust proof preferably.

STITCHES USED IN ELIZABETHAN EMBROIDERY

Embroidery has a rich tradition of stitches to draw upon. Frequently embroiderers use but a limited repertoire of stitches, ignoring the wealth of different stitches that have been used in the past. This book gives you the opportunity to expand your stitch vocabulary with instructions for some of the stitches which were in common use a few hundred years ago!

HANDY HINT
If you find any of the stitches a little difficult to master, practise working the stitch using heavier thread, for example DMC Perle 5, when you have mastered the technique it will be easy to transfer to using a finer thread.

Chain Stitch

actual size 10 - 12 stitches per inch

fig. 1

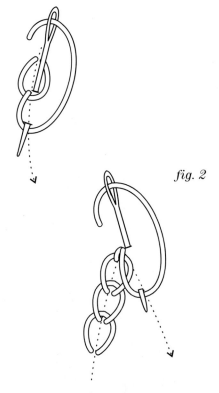

fig. 2

Chain stitch is the most frequently used stitch in Elizabethan embroidery. It is used to outline all shapes worked in the designs in this book and it is always worked first with only one exception, the strawberry. Chain stitch is worked around the strawberry last to neaten the outside edge.

The chain stitch must be kept small and even as subsequently many other stitches are worked into the initial chain stitch outline. It is worked using a No. 8 crewel or embroidery needle (fig. 1).

How to stitch a sharp point in chain stitch

In Elizabethan Embroidery further stitches are usually worked into the chain stitch outline of the shapes so it is most important to be able to work chain stitch to create a nice point. Rounded 'points' on a bud or calyx would ruin the appearance of your flower.

Chain stitch to the point, then take the thread from the chain at the tip of the point through to the back of the work. To anchor the chain do a small back stitch at the back of your work then bring the needle through to the front *at the same place you went down* and continue chain stitching away from the point. Try to have the two sides of the point with an equal number of stitches up to and away from the point so that you can work subsequent stitches evenly (fig. 2).

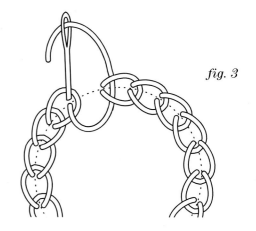

fig. 3

HOW TO CHAIN STITCH A COMPLETE CIRCLE

Stitch round the circle until you are just one stitch from joining the beginning of the circle then take the needle under both threads of the first chain as shown taking the needle through to the back of the material just beside the point where your thread came out from the last chain in the circle (fig. 3).

SPINE CHAIN

Spine chain stitch is created by working a basic chain stitch (fig. 1), followed by a straight stitch worked at an angle from the chain (fig. 2). The needle is then brought back up as shown and the next chain stitch is worked (fig.3).

fig. 1

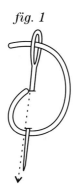

fig. 2

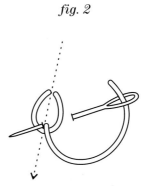

fig. 3

CABLE CHAIN

I use this stitch sometimes when I need to emphasise the line around a design shape. When this stitch is worked in gold it is a most effective and attractive line stitch.

Work a normal chain stitch then lay your work down on a table or your lap and hold the thread between the finger and thumb of the left hand and place the needle *under* the thread (fig. 1).

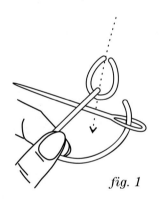
fig. 1

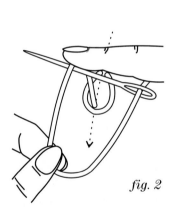
fig. 2

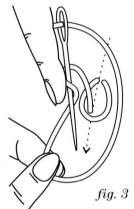
fig. 3

fig. 4

The next step is very important, lift the thread in your left hand *high* and place your right finger on top of the thread on the needle (fig. 2).
Now twist the needle over the top of the thread ready to make another chain, still keeping your finger on the thread, which is resting on the needle (fig. 3).

Insert needle into work - a little in front of previous chain, the thread will be slack, now pull the thread down on the needle to form the 'cable', *before* pulling the needle through the fabric to create the next chain stitch (fig. 4).

LACED CHAIN

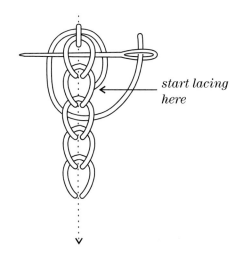

start lacing here

A line of chain stitch is worked finishing with a little straight stitch to anchor the last chain down. With the straight stitch at the top of your work take a thread of a different colour and bring your needle out beside the line of chain stitch two chains down from where you finished. Take the thread up to the straight stitch and thread the needle under the straight stitch, bring the thread down three chains (so that it is now one in front of where you started) and take the thread under the chain.

Now take the thread back up two chain stitches and thread the needle under the chain stitch, bring the thread down three chains and continue as before, gradually working your way down the line of chain stitch. The looped thread can be left as large or small as required depending on the size of the leaf you are working on. When you are ready to finish hold the last loop made carefully between your finger and thumb, take the needle through to the back of the work beside the last chain stitch and do a back stitch to anchor your thread.

HANDY HINT

This stitch can be used most effectively when working larger leaves when both the outline and the central row of chain stitch can be laced.

It also looks most attractive with the loops pulled tight on one side but not on the other.

PLAITED STITCH

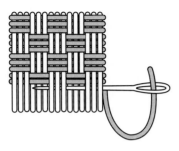

Plaited stitch is a decorative darning stitch which does need to be worked in a frame.

It is created by stitching vertical rows of satin stitch to cover the entire shape, then horizontal rows of darning stitch are worked in a contrasting colour.

The vertical rows of satin stitch need to be worked very neatly with each stitch close to the last and covering the entire area. Try to keep the edges even. With thread of a contrasting colour work the horizontal rows of stitching darning over and under three rows of the vertical stitching, take thread right back to beginning to start the next row of darning. Every three rows alternate the threads picked up.

Traditionally, when threads were not as freely available as they are now, this stitch was worked with all the thread on the surface, so that at the end of each row the needle was taken through to the back and brought back to the surface just one thread along from where the needle was taken down. The modern method where it is stitched like satin stitch is easier!

RAISED KNOT

This stitch is also called Square Boss Stitch

Coloured silk embroidery in the Elizabethan period was very rich in texture and colour and there were few empty spaces! I use this stitch to enrich an area where beads or sequins are not appropriate but additional detail is necessary.

First a cross stitch is worked then each arm of the cross stitch is covered with a back stitch to make a firm raised knot.

fig. 1  *fig. 2*  *fig. 3*  *fig. 4*

HANDY HINT
If a space looks a little bare and a bead is not right, work a number of these little knots.

LADDER STITCH

I personally favour the use of this stitch for all coiling stems. It creates a good broad border with a heavy textured edge. It may also be worked into a leaf shape and when surrounded with chain stitch it gives a most interesting variation for a leaf.

It is well worth persevering to master this stitch. You may find working a leaf first is a good way to practise the technique. As the name states there is a space between each rung of a 'ladder'. If the stitch is 'jammed up' too closely to the above bar, the line becomes wobbly and an uneven appearance develops. It is hard to work effectively in tight scrolls so for that reason I work all the very fine tendrils in chain stitch.

You may replace ladder stitch with two rows of chain stitch, with the centre loops of each of the chain stitch rows whipped together, one row of chain stitch and one row of stem stitch worked side by side, or one row of chain and one row of stem worked side by side with one side of the chain stitch and the stem stitch whipped together.

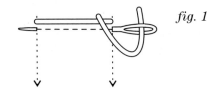

fig. 1

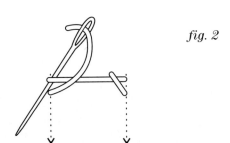

fig. 2

WORKING LADDER STITCH

Step 1   Work a straight stitch first and come up above it on the right hand side as shown. Then take a second straight stitch beneath the first bringing the needle out directly beneath the first stitch (fig. 1).

Step 2   Take the needle through the first straight stitch you worked, on the left hand side (not picking up the material only the thread) as shown (fig. 2). Pull thread firm but not tight.

Step 3   Loop the thread across to the right hand side and pass the needle under the straight stitch and the angled stitch on the right hand side. (Don't pick up the material - just the thread.) Leave the thread a little slack (fig. 3).

fig. 3

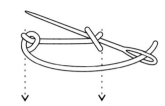

Step 4   Now take the needle through the fabric from right to left as shown, do not take this stitch too close to the above stitching (fig. 4).

fig. 4

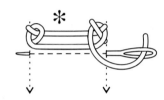

Step 5   Lift up and slide the needle under the chain on the left hand side (fig. 5). Pull firmly here.

fig. 5

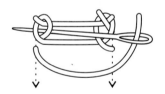

Step 6   Loop thread across to the right hand side and life up and slide needle under the chain on the right hand side (fig. 6). Now repeat step 4, taking the needle across from the right to the left through the fabric. Steps 4, 5, and 6 *-*are repeated to continue this stitch.

fig. 6

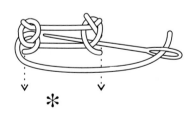

HANDY HINT
The needle must be kept horizontal and always pointing in the same direction.

HANDY RHYME
To remember what to do once you have got started
"lift up on the left,
lift up on the right -
take a bite".

DETACHED BUTTONHOLE

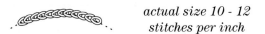

actual size 10 - 12 stitches per inch

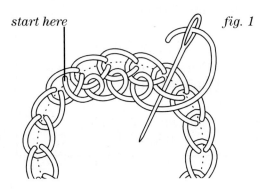

start here   *fig. 1*

fig. 2

This stitch has tremendous creative possibilities. Flowers, leaves, pansies, blossoms and pea pods are all worked most successfully using this stitch. It is important when you are working detached buttonhole stitch that the stitching is parallel with the base. If this stitch is not worked as shown it makes working 'lifted up' detached buttonhole on the petal at a later stage most difficult.

To work detached buttonhole stitch the entire shape to be filled must be outlined with small neat chain stitches using a No. 8 embroidery or crewel needle.

Detached buttonhole stitch is worked in one direction - from left to right. The thread is returned from right to left with a long straight stitch. Always work detached buttonhole stitch from the outer edge of the petal towards the centre.

To start, using a No. 24 tapestry needle, bring the thread to the front at the top left hand corner as shown, from this point the needle does not enter the material again until finishing. Work detached buttonhole stitch across the row of chains only working into the lower loop of the chain stitch (fig. 1).

At the right hand side the needle is taken *under and up* into the inner loop of the chain stitch then the thread is taken back across the work to the left hand side where it goes *under* then *up* into the inner chain stitch loop of the left hand side on the shape. Now continue working detached buttonhole stitch into each loop of the stitch above and catching the straight thread underneath as well (fig. 2). Do not catch the fabric.

UP AND DOWN BUTTONHOLE

This stitch gives a most interesting textural variation to your work.

To work up and down buttonhole stitch, once again the entire shape to be filled must first be outlined with small neat chain stitches using a No. 8 crewel or embroidery needle. Always start stitching up and down buttonhole on the outside edge of the flower petal and work towards the flower centre.

Up and down buttonhole stitch is worked in one direction - from left to right. The thread is returned from right to left with a long straight stitch. Keep the thread firm but do not pull tight.

To start, bring the thread to the front at the top on the left hand side using a No. 24 tapestry needle (fig. 1). From this point the needle does not enter the material again until finishing.

Work the up and down buttonhole stitches across the row of chains only working into the lower loop of the chain stitch. *One up* and *one down* buttonhole stitch is worked into each chain (fig.2).

At the right hand side the needle is taken *under* and *up* into the inner loop of the chain stitch then the thread is taken back across the work to the left hand side where it goes *under* then *up* into the inner chain stitch loop of the left hand side of the shape. Now continue working up and down buttonhole stitch by slipping the needle *behind the loop that is between* the pairs of buttonhole stitches also catching the straight thread beneath. Do not catch the fabric.

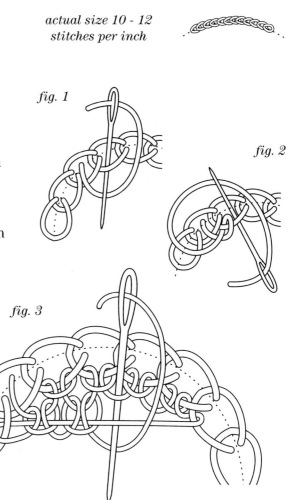

actual size 10 - 12 stitches per inch

fig. 1

fig. 2

fig. 3

TRELLIS STITCH

*actual size 10 - 12
stitches per inch*

Trellis stitch was used frequently in the Elizabethan period. It is a knotted, surface stitch which curves beautifully. It is worked both from left to right and on the return row, from right to left. Interesting effects can be obtained by changing the colour of the thread while stitching.

To work trellis stitch, the entire shape to be filled must be outlined with chain stitch using a crewel No. 8 needle. Note our diagram showing the actual size to work chain stitch. Trellis stitch can be worked either starting from the outer edge of the shape working towards the centre or it can be stitched lengthwise to follow the chain stitch outline as it does in the pomegranate.

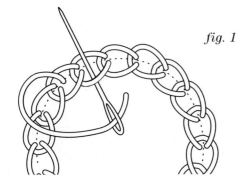

fig. 1

FIRST ROW

Change to a tapestry No 24 needle and bring it out in the top left hand chain on the left hand side. From this point the needle does not enter the material again until finishing.

The needle is slipped *under and up* into the next chain, pull the needle through leaving a loop of thread (fig.1).

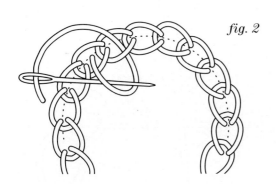

fig. 2

Now slip the needle from the left *under and up* into the loose loop, pull towards the left first and then to the right to tighten. Repeat the last two steps into every chain until the end is reached (fig.2).

RETURN JOURNEY

You are now ready to work back across the row. Bring needle *under and up* into the chain on right hand side.

Slip needle *under and up* into the thread between the knots in the row above, pull the needle through leaving a loop of thread (fig. 3).

Now slip the needle from the right *under and up* into the loop, pull towards the right then to the left to create a knot. This row is worked from right to left (fig. 4).

The third row, worked from left to right, the needle slips *under and up* into the loops between the knots on the previous row.

fig. 3

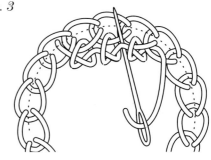

fig. 4

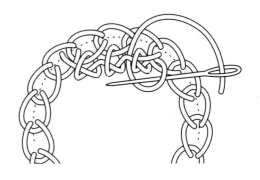

HANDY HINT

This stitch can become a little stretchy if care is not taken to work the initial row of chain stitch in small, not tiny, neat stitches. Chain stitches which are too large will make the stitch stretchy and full of holes.

Lifted up Detached Buttonhole

actual size 10 - 12 stitches per inch

The three dimensional effect created using this technique gives great charm and instant eye appeal to your embroidery.

Lifting up a petal always begins in the same manner. Firstly the the area must be completely covered with detached buttonhole stitch which has been padded a little in the usual way. The wadding raises the stitching a little making the lines of stitching easier to see.

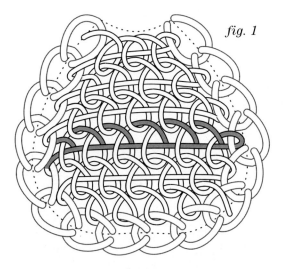

fig. 1

With the completed petal as the base, thread a sharp pointed needle (crewel No. 8) with thread to match the colour of the petal beneath and start to work buttonhole stitch approximately halfway down on the petal. (After you have worked the first row it is easier if you continue stitching using a tapestry needle.)

When working the lifted up detached buttonhole you work *from the middle of the worked petal towards the outer edge* of the petal (fig.1).

Bring the needle out in the chain stitch at the left hand edge of the petal. Work buttonhole stitch across the width of the petal working into each loop and bar with the last stitch into the chain stitch on the right hand side (fig. 2). Hold the work so that you are working towards the outer edge of the petal. (It can be useful to hold your thumb under the stitches you are working to keep them separate from the stitching on the petal.)

Note the petal has been inverted to show that you work from the middle towards the outside edge when working lifted up detached buttonhole stitch.

When you have reached the right hand edge the thread is looped across to the left hand side, bring your needle *under* then *up* into the loop of the first buttonhole stitch you worked on the left hand side. Leave the thread a little loose, but keep it out of the way until you have inserted your needle into the loop of your first buttonhole stitch. Now tighten thread and work buttonhole stitch across the row *in loops formed in the row above* and down under the straight thread you brought across. From now on the work is executed in the air. Continue to work your rows of buttonhole stitch into the loops of the row above and down over the looped thread. Take care to keep the rows worked now, separate from the base embroidery. Continue in this manner until shaping is needed.

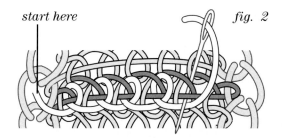

start here   *fig. 2*

The darkened threads shown indicate the threads you will pick up to start your first row of lifted up detached buttonhole stitch

TO KEEP THE SIDES STRAIGHT

Work your first buttonhole stitch in the second row directly beneath the first buttonhole stitch worked in the first row and your last stitch directly beneath the last in the first row.

TO INCREASE IN LIFTED UP DETACHED BUTTONHOLE STITCH

At times you will need to increase or decrease using this stitch to make sure your lifted up petal is the same shape as the one beneath.

To increase, at the beginning of a new row work two buttonhole stitches into the first loop and again into the last loop at the end of the row. Sometimes it is necessary to increase in the centre of a lifted up petal. To do this two stitches are worked into one loop in the centre (fig. 3).

To Increase

fig. 3

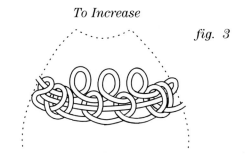

An extra buttonhole stitch is worked at the beginning and end of the row, and if necessary an extra stitch could be worked in the centre also.

To Decrease

fig. 4

TO DECREASE

Finish the row, loop the thread across to the left as before into the first stitch but *do not* put the needle back into this same loop - work the first stitch this row into the next loop. Work across to the end, Do not work into the last stitch at the end of the row, work your last stitch into the *second to last* loop.

If you wished to create a lifted up point you would continue decreasing in the same way until a point had been created.

TO FINISH OFF

To neaten the working thread when you have completed the lifted up buttonhole petal just whip down the side of the petal until the base of the lifted portion of the petal is reached. Take thread to the back of the work, anchor with a couple of little back stitches. The lifted up petal nearly always curls on the right hand side when the petal is complete.

TO FINISH OR CHANGE THREAD COLOUR
IN THE MIDDLE OF STITCHING A PETAL IN LIFTED UP DETACHED BUTTONHOLE STITCH

When you want to start or finish threads, or change to a different colour in the middle of a petal, the old thread is whipped down the side of the petal and then taken through to the back and anchored. Bring in the new colour on the right hand edge of the lifted up petal work a little back stitch on the lifted up petal, now loop this thread across in the usual manner and continue working detached buttonhole with the new coloured thread. The start of your new colour is covered with buttonhole stitch so that the threads are firmly secured and your starting point hidden.

HANDY HINTS
- Always start a new lifted up petal with a new thread.
- To create an even richer effect slip stitch or buttonhole stitch in gold thread around the petals after they have all been completed.

OTHER STITCHES USED

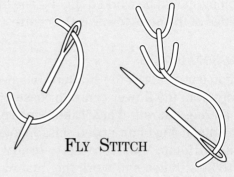 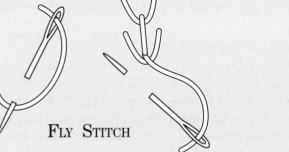

FLY STITCH

STRAIGHT STITCH

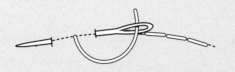

BACK STITCH

FEATHER STITCH

SATIN STITCH

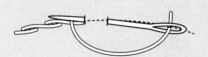

STEM STITCH

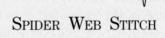

SPIDER WEB STITCH

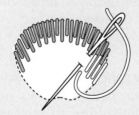

LONG AND SHORT STITCH

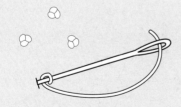

FRENCH KNOT STITCH

Shape Section

Now that you have mastered some new stitch techniques it is time to use these stitches to embroider the beautiful flowers we give directions for in our shape section

fig 1

On each of the shapes we show by arrows the position to start working the filling stitches from and the angle at which the stitching should be worked (fig. 1). The filling stitches are usually worked from the outer edge of the petal towards the centre.

Padding and closing petals

This work is very textural. The texture is created not only by the stitching but also by a little padding. When you are one row away from the flower centre or base of the petal, depending on the shape you are embroidering, stop stitching. Take a small piece of very soft dacron padding, roll it into a ball and using blunt-nosed scissors push it high up inside the shape - do not make it into a hard lump. Make sure there are no wisps of dacron sticking down into the area yet to be stitched and work the final row of filling stitch.

When you are filling a petal shape and working back to a centre as for example with the pansy or blossom, it is important to keep the centre as a feature. Slip stitch the completed petal down to the fabric right up close to the chain stitch but not actually going though it. When you have filled a petal for example like the cornflower where the calyx outline is not a feature slip stitch the completed petal down into the centre of the chain outline to maintain uniformity with the rest of the flower.

After closing the petal spread the dacron out with your needle so that there are no hard lumps and the padding is soft and even.

Padding and closing leaves

Leaves are padded in the same way as petals by pushing a little ball of dacron up into the tip of the petal with blunt-nosed scissors. After the leaf is padded it is closed by slip stitching it down at the base of the leaf into the centre of the chain outline. As you have worked your filling stitches into the inner edge of the chain stitch outline by closing off into the inner edge of chain stitch your leaf will have a nice even outer edge.

Changing colours

Elizabethan needlewomen frequently changed colours when they were stitching and it is very easy to do. With detached buttonhole and up and down buttonhole finish the row, take your thread to the back and neaten off. Bring your new thread to the front on the *right hand side* loop across to left and carry on stitching normally.

When working trellis stitch start a new colour at either end of a row.

Stitching a curved petal

When you have a petal with an indented outer edge you have to do extra stitching in each of the curved sections. Start your filling stitch at the outer edge of the curve on the left hand side. Stop when you have filled in that section. Move to the outer edge of the curve on the right hand side and with the same needle and thread work until you have completed that section, still using the same needle and thread now work across the whole area always keeping the stitching parallel to the base (fig. 1). Sometimes it can be helpful to draw lines onto your fabric (use a hard pencil, water erasable pen or fine tip spirit marker) as a guide and remember beads can be used most successfully to cover the odd 'glitch'.

fig 1

Stitching a Curved Petal

Stitching into points

A number of the leaves and flowers have quite tight points which need to be stitched neatly, keeping the points sharp, to look attractive.

Start stitching your filling stitch at the tip of the point on the left hand side. Stop at the bottom of the 'V'(fig. 2). Move to the tip in the centre with the same needle and thread and work down to the bottom of that shape, stop. Repeat in the same manner with the third tip then work with the same needle and thread across the whole area.

fig 2

Stitching into Points

FINISHING OFF

Take thread through to the back and neaten off with a little back stitch or two.

FOXGLOVE

All chain and feather stitch to be worked using a crewel No. 8 needle.
All detached buttonhole and trellis stitch to be worked using a tapestry No. 22 - 26 needle.
Arrows indicate where to start stitching and the direction in which to stitch rows.
For best results we recommend you stitch the foxglove in the sequence given.

STEMS, BRANCH AND TENDRIL

Chain stitch in 840.

CALYX

Outline in chainstitch with 801. *Starting at the left hand tip* fill the area with detached buttonhole stitch worked using 840 and multi-coloured metallic thread in the needle together worked as one. Pad a little and close at the base. Detailed instructions on how to work pointed areas are given on page 33.

FLOWER

Both flowers are worked in the same way, chain stitch round the main part of each flower using 3328. Then work in trellis stitch filling the area with three bands of colour *starting at the outer edge* with 3328 then changing to 3326 and finally to 754. Pad a little and close. Refer to the diagram for the variation in the shading or refer to the colour photograph on page 51.

OUTER LIP

Outline in chain stitch and *starting at the outer edge* fill with detached buttonhole using 369. Pad a little and close then stitch a sprinkling of rust coloured bugle beads in this area to add a little sparkle.

LEAVES

All three are worked in the same way. Outline in chain stitch using 904. *Starting at the tip of the leaf* fill with detached buttonhole stitch using 369. Pad a little and close. Vein markings have been worked in feather stitch using gold metallic thread.

THREADS - COTON A BRODER 16
369   light green
754   soft pink
801   dark brown
840   medium brown
904   apple green
3326   pink
3328   coral
gold and multi-coloured metallic thread

colour change ············
1st row of chain ——————
2nd row of chain – – – – –
3rd row of chain ············

start stitching here ⟶
direction of rows ⟷

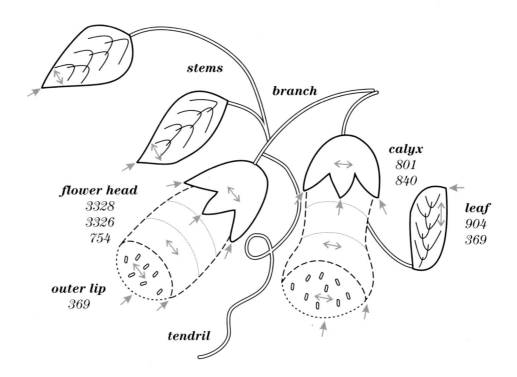

stems

branch

calyx
801
840

flower head
3328
3326
754

leaf
904
369

outer lip
369

tendril

*stems, branch and tendril to
be chain stitched in 840*

35

CORNFLOWER

All chain stitch to be worked using a crewel No. 8 needle.
All detached buttonhole stitch to be worked using a tapestry No. 22 - 26 needle.
Arrows indicate where to start stitching and the direction in which to stitch rows.
For best results we recommend you stitch the cornflower in the sequence given.

STEMS AND TENDRILS

Chain stitch stems and tendrils using 840.

CALYX

Outline in chain stitch and *starting at the tips* fill with detached buttonhole stitch worked in 469. Detailed instructions on how to work pointed areas are given on page 33.

PETALS

The petals are outlined in chain stitch with 797. *Starting at the outer edge* of the petal, work in detached buttonhole stitch filling each petal with three bands of colour changing from dark, 797 at the outer edge to 799 in the middle area and light, 800 at the centre. Do *not* pad. Refer to the diagram for the variations in the shading of the petals or refer to the colour photograph on page 51. Detailed instructions on how to change colours are given on page 33. To complete the cornflower, sew a sprinkling of little blue beads where indicated.

THREADS - COTON A BRODER 16
469   olive green
797   royal blue
799   medium blue
800   light blue
840   medium brown

HANDY HINT
If you feel an area is not stitched quite as neatly as you would like, sew a few beads here over your stitching

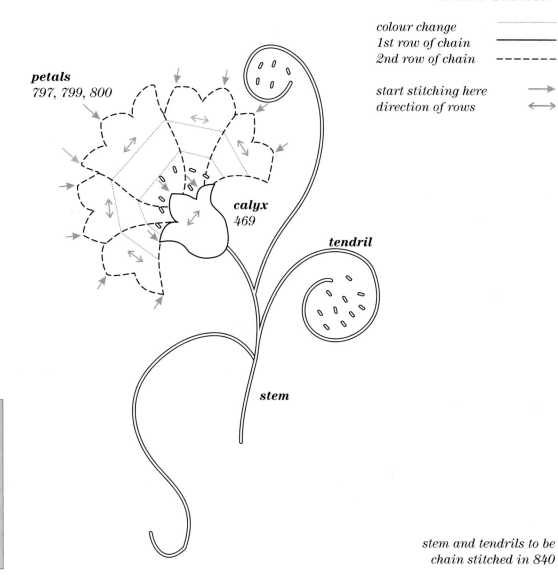

colour change
1st row of chain
2nd row of chain

start stitching here →
direction of rows ↔

petals
797, 799, 800

calyx
469

tendril

stem

HANDY HINT
When you are stitching the petals you will work the detached buttonhole stitch from one petal into one side of the chain and the detached buttonhole from the next petal into the other side of the chain.

stem and tendrils to be chain stitched in 840

PRIMROSES

THREADS - COTON A BRODER 16

301   rust
469   olive green
471   light olive green
727   citrus yellow
743   yellow
840   medium brown
945   peach
yellow stranded cotton
Note variation in colours of petals

All chain and satin stitch to be worked using a crewel No. 8 needle.
All detached buttonhole stitch and laced chain stitching is to be worked using a tapestry No. 22 - 26 needle.
Arrows indicate where to start stitching and the direction in which to stitch rows.
For best results we recommend you stitch the primrose in the sequence given.

STEM, TENDRILS AND SEED PODS

Chain stitch stems and tendrils using 840 and satin stitch each seed pod using three threads of matching yellow stranded cotton.

FLOWER CENTRES

Outline in chain stitch using 301 and highlight with a sequin sewn in the centre.

PETALS

Outline each petal in chain stitch using the colour to match subsequent stitching. *Starting at the outer edge,* sew the petals in detached buttonhole stitch, refer to the diagram for the variations in the petal colours. Pad each petal with a little dacron before closing.

FLORAL TUBE

Work chain stitch around shape and in a straight line down the centre using 471. Work laced chain down the centre line of chain stitch using 469.

1st row of chain ⎯⎯⎯⎯
2nd row of chain ⎯ ⎯ ⎯ ⎯
3rd row of chain ⋯⋯⋯⋯⋯

start stitching here →
direction of rows ↔

petals
727, 743, 945

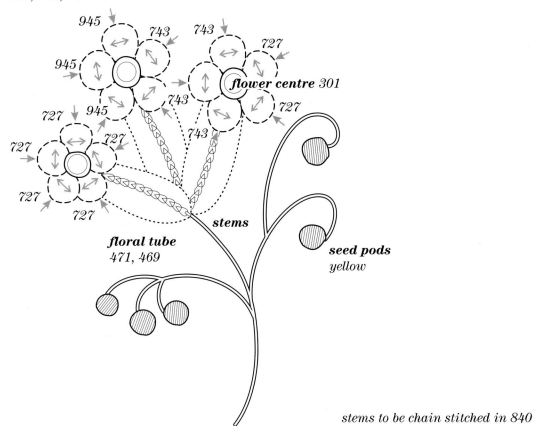

945

743 *743*

945 *727*

flower centre *301*

727 *945* *743* *727*

727 *727* *743*

727 *727* **stems**

727

floral tube
471, 469

seed pods
yellow

stems to be chain stitched in 840

Daffodil

Threads - Coton a broder 16

101   variegated green
701   bright green
702   light bright green
740   orange
742   dark yellow
743   yellow
840   medium brown
gold and multi-coloured metallic thread

All chain and stem stitch to be worked using a crewel No. 8 needle.
All detached buttonhole and trellis stitch to be worked using a tapestry
No. 22 - 26 needle.
Arrows indicate where to start stitching and the direction in which to stitch rows.
For best results we recommend you stitch the daffodil in the sequence given.

Stem of Daffodil

Chain stitch the stem using 701 and then whip with 743.

Trumpet

Chain stitch the outline of the trumpet and the two dividing lines inside the trumpet using 740. *Starting at the outer edge* of the trumpet work *along* the shape still using 740 fill the three areas with trellis stitch. There is no need to pad these sections. Work chain stitch in gold metallic thread up the two dividing lines inside the trumpet.

Petals

Outline each petal in chain stitch with the colour to be used in subsequent stitching, refer to the diagram for the variations in colours used on the petals. *Starting at the tip of each petal*, work detached buttonhole stitch in all petals. When stitching the two petals using 742, thread multi-coloured metallic thread in your needle with the coton a broder and work the threads as one. This will give your work an extra 'glitter'. Do *not* pad any of these petals.

Left Hand Leaf

Outline in chain stitch and *starting where indicated on the lower edge* work across the leaf shape filling the area with detached buttonhole stitch using 701. Pad a little before closing.

LARGE RIGHT HAND LEAF

Outline in chain stitch and *starting at the point on the inner edge* work across the leaf shape filling the area with detached buttonhole stitch using 702. Pad a little before closing.

SMALL RIGHT HAND LEAF

Outline in chain stitch, then *starting at the tip* fill with detached buttonhole stitch using 101. Pad a little before closing. The stem has been worked in chain stitch using 840, still using 840 work the vein markings on the leaf in stem stitch to complete.

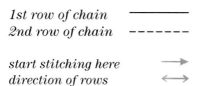

1st row of chain ⎯⎯⎯⎯
2nd row of chain – – – – –

start stitching here →
direction of rows ↔

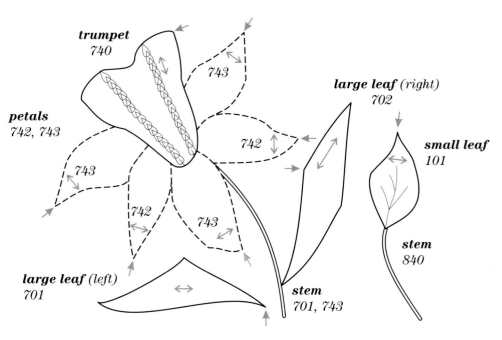

trumpet
740

petals
742, 743

743

742

743

742

743

large leaf (*left*)
701

stem
701, 743

large leaf (*right*)
702

small leaf
101

stem
840

stems to be chain stitched using colours indicated on diagram

41

Blossom

Threads - Coton a broder 16

48   variegated pink
469   olive green
471   light olive green
840   medium brown
3689 light raspberry pink
ecru
gold metallic thread

All chain and buttonhole stitch to be worked using a crewel No. 8 needle.
All laced chain and detached and lifted up detached buttonhole stitch to be worked using a tapestry No. 22 - 26 needle.
Arrows indicate where to start stitching and the direction in which to stitch rows.
For best results we recommend you stitch the blossom in the sequence given.

Stems
These are worked in chain stitch using 840.

Flower Centre
Chain stitch round the centre edge using 469 and sew a pearl bead in the centre to complete.

Petals
Outline all petals in chain stitch with the colour used in subsequent stitching. Petals can be stitched using two or three shades, this gives added interest to the embroidery and can be worked to suit your taste.

Start stitching at the outer edge of the petal, work towards the centre of the flower and fill each petal with detached buttonhole stitch. Refer to the diagram for the variations in the petal colours. Pad each petal a little before closing.

Lifted Up Petals
Lifted up petals are stitched in the same variations of thread as the petals beneath. Remember to start at about the middle of the petal and work *towards the outer* edge. Edge with buttonhole stitch using gold metallic thread.

Filaments
Embroider lines extending from between each petal of the blossom in chain stitch using 469. Sew a little white pearl bead at the end of each filament.

Bud

Outline in chain stitch and *starting at the tip* fill with detached buttonhole stitch using 48, pad a little before closing. Still using 48 sew three straight stitches extending from the tip of the bud and sew a small white pearl at the end of each extension.

Leaf

Outline with chain stitch using 471, then work a straight row of chain stitch down the centre, work laced chain down the centre line of chain stitch still using 471.

1st row of chain ————
2nd row of chain - - - - - - -

start stitching here →
direction of rows ↔

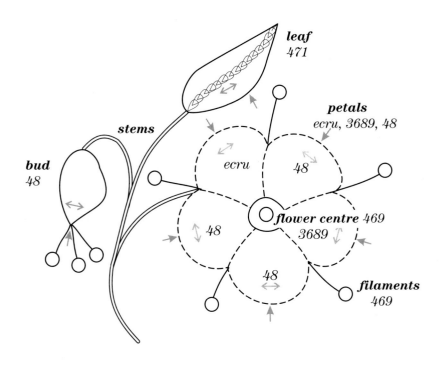

leaf
471

petals
ecru, 3689, 48

stems

bud
48

ecru

48

flower centre 469
3689

48

48

48

filaments
469

stems to be chain stitched in 840

PANSY

THREADS - COTON A BRODER 16

101   variegated green
552   purple
553   medium purple
702   light bright green
743   yellow
840   medium brown
904   apple green
gold metallic thread
green stranded cotton

All chain, stem and fly stitch to be worked using a crewel No. 8 needle.
All detached and up and down buttonhole to be stitched using a tapestry
No. 22 - 26 needle.
Arrows indicate where to start stitching and the direction in which to stitch rows.
For best results we recommend you stitch the pansy in the sequence given.

PANSY AND BUD STEM

The stems going up to the pansy flower, upper and lower buds, and leaf by the upper bud are to be worked in chain stitch using 904. The other stem is to be worked in chain stitch using 840.

FLOWER CENTRE

Chain stitch around the centre edge using 743. To complete sew a gold sequin held in place with a small bead.

PETALS

Outline the lower petal in chain stitch using 743 and then fill area with up and down buttonhole stitch worked in the same colour. *Start at the lower edge of the petal* and work towards the centre, pad a little before closing.

Outline the two side petals in chain stitch using 553 then using up and down buttonhole *work from the outer edge towards the centre*, working firstly in 553, then change about half way to 743 to complete the petals. Pad before closing.

Outline the two upper petals in chain stitch using 552 then still using 552 work detached buttonhole stitch *from the outer edge* finishing at the centre. Do not pad these petals.

As a finishing touch work long straight stitches radiating out from the centre on the two side petals and the lower petal using gold metallic thread. Refer to the diagram for details or the colour plate on page 51.

PIN CUSHIONS

THE SAMPLER

detached buttonhole is shown on pages 29 - 30. Catch it down at the top and shape at the bottom. Whip along the edge of the flap using gold metallic thread.

PEAS

The peas are worked separately in trellis stitch on a small piece of linen, and then stitched to the embroidery when completed. Take your fabric and using 562 work a single chain stitch on it. Now work trellis stitch into the outer loops of the chain stitch initially and subsequently between the bars into the row of trellis stitch above.

To ensure that your work lies flat, increase as you stitch. Increases are made by working twice between the same bar when required. Work round and round in circles until you have covered an area of about 1 cm in diameter. When you have reached the required size work a running stitch around the edge of your stitching, cut away from fabric (there will be a little scrap under the original chain stitch) pull up into a ball, then attach to completed pea pod shape.

LEAF TO THE LEFT OF THE PEA POD

Outline leaf in chain stitch using 561. Still using 561 *work from the outer edge* of the leaf towards the central vein in detached buttonhole stitch, changing at the centre to 562 to complete the leaf. Pad a little and close. A central vein has been worked in stem stitch using 562.

LEAF TO THE RIGHT OF THE PEA POD

Outline leaf in chain stitch using 562. Still using 562 *work from the outer edge* of the leaf towards the central vein in detached buttonhole stitch, changing at the centre to 504 to complete the leaf. Pad a little and close. A central vein has been worked in stem stitch using 840.

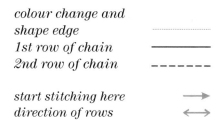

colour change and
shape edge ··········
1st row of chain ————
2nd row of chain - - - - - -

start stitching here →
direction of rows ↔

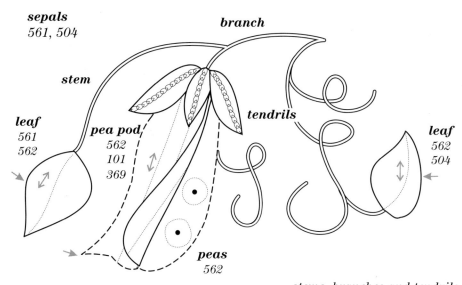

sepals
561, 504

branch

stem

leaf
561
562

pea pod
562
101
369

tendrils

leaf
562
504

peas
562

*stems, branches and tendrils
to be chain stitched in 840*

49

Honeysuckle

All chain and stem stitch to be worked using a crewel No. 8 needle.
All detached buttonhole stitch to be worked using a tapestry No. 22 - 26 needle.
Arrows indicate where to start stitching and the direction in which to stitch rows.
For best results we recommend you stitch the honeysuckle in the sequence given.

Stems

All stems are chain stitched in 840.

Flower Centre

Chain stitch around the edge of the circle in 727 then sew a sequin with a little bead on top to complete the centre.

Petals

Outline all the petals in chain stitch using 782. Still using 782 work detached buttonhole stitch *starting at the outer edge* of the petal, change about half way to 727 to complete each petal. Pad a little before closing. Refer to the diagram for the variation in the shading of the honeysuckle or refer to the colour photograph on page 51.

Seed between each petal

Outline the seed in chain stitch using 782 then fill area with detached buttonhole stitch worked in 211 *starting at the outer curve.* Pad a little before closing.

Three Buds

Top left bud - All yellow - outline in chain stitch then fill with detached buttonhole stitch using 727 throughout.
Lower left hand bud - Bud with pink base and yellow top - outline in chain stitch using 727 and then with the same thread work detached buttonhole stitch to cover half the area changing to 224 to complete the bud.
Right hand side bud - Bud with yellow base and pink top - outline with chain stitch using 224 and then with the same thread work detached buttonhole stitch to cover half

Threads - Coton a broder 16

211   mauve
224   medium Paris pink
469   olive green
727   citrus yellow
782   mustard
840   medium brown
multi-coloured metallic thread

'Swete Bage'

THE CAT

WOODLAND NYMPH

SERVIETTE RINGS

EVENING BAG

SHIRLEY HOLDAWAY

SHIRLEY HOLDAWAY

PATRICIA BOTTOMLEY

J. LESTER

IRENE McDAIRMID

ROSE LANCASTER

SHIRLEY HOLDAWAY

V. GARRETT

DOROTHY CLARKE

HEATHER WALKER

LILIANE ASHFORTH

BERNICE MILLS

JANET MITCHELL

the area, before changing to 727 to complete the bud. None of the buds have any padding. Small yellow/gold beads have been sewn on the buds where indicated.

LEAVES

These are both worked in the same way. Outline in chain stitch then *starting at the tip* fill with detached buttonhole stitch using 469 and multi-coloured metallic thread in the needle together, worked as one. Pad a little and close. Work a straight line of stem stitch using 840 to indicate the central veins.

colour change ....
1st row of chain ──────
2nd row of chain ‒ ‒ ‒ ‒ ‒
3rd row of chain ....

start stitching here ⟶
direction of rows ⟷

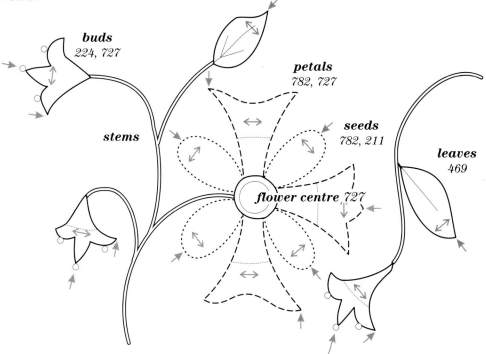

buds
224, 727

petals
782, 727

stems

seeds
782, 211

leaves
469

flower centre 727

stems to be chain stitched in 840

POMEGRANATE

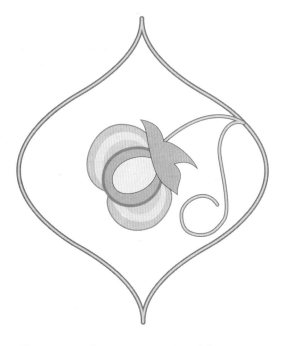

THREADS - COTON A BRODER 16

223 Paris pink
224 medium Paris pink
562 mint green
815 ruby red
840 medium brown
945 peach
3032 taupe
multi-coloured metallic thread

All chain stitches to be worked using a crewel No. 8 needle.
All detached buttonhole and trellis stitch to be worked using a tapestry No. 22-26 needle.
Arrows indicate where to start stitching and the direction in which to stitch rows.
Note that trellis stitch follows *along* the line of chain stitch in the flesh and skin areas of the pomegranate but is worked *across* the area in the seed. Refer to the diagram for further detail.
For best results we recommend you stitch the pomegranate in the sequence given.

STEM AND TENDRILS

These are to be chain stitched using 840.

CALYX

Outline calyx in chain stitch using 562. *Starting at the upper point* fill the area with detached buttonhole stitch worked using 562 and multi-coloured metallic thread in the needle together worked as one. Pad a little and close.

SEED

Outline central seed in chain stitch and fill area with trellis stitch worked using 945. *Starting stitching at the calyx* and work down.

FLESH

Work chain stitch in 815 on next curved line. Between these two rows of chain stitch (the first on the edge of the seed and the second you have just worked) the area is filled with trellis stitch. *Starting at the inner curve* and working *along* the line of chain stitch, not across, fill this area with trellis stitch using 223. Pad a little before closing.

SKIN

Chain stitch round outer line using 223. Fill this area with trellis stitch using 224 on the edges but working two rows of 223 down the centre. Once again work trellis stitch *along* the line of chain stitch, not *across*. Pad a little before closing. Refer to the colour photograph on page 51 for additional detail.

colour change ....

1st row of chain —————

2nd row of chain — — — —

3rd row of chain ············

4th row of chain —·—·—·—

direction of stitching ⟶

direction of rows ⟷

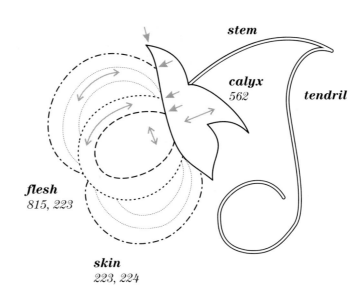

stem

calyx
562

tendril

flesh
815, 223

skin
223, 224

*stem and tendril to be
chain stitched in 840*

GRAPES

All chain and stem stitch to be worked using a crewel No. 8 needle.

All detached buttonhole and trellis stitch to be worked using a tapestry No. 22 - 26 needle.

Arrows indicate where to start stitching and the direction in which to stitch rows. For best results we recommend you stitch the grapes in the sequence given.

STEM AND TENDRILS

The stem and tendrils are worked in chain stitch using 840.

LEAF

Outline in chain stitch using 561. Working in detached buttonhole stitch and using 101 *start at the left hand tip* of the leaf filling each point first then fill the rest of the leaf area. Detailed instructions on how to work pointed areas are given on page 33. Pad a little and close. Work the veins in stem stitch using gold metallic thread.

GRAPES

The grapes are worked separately on a small piece of linen in trellis stitch and then stitched to the embroidery when completed. (They are worked in the same way as the peas on the pea pod.) The grapes are shaded using 336, 552 and 792, refer to the diagram for the variation in the shading of the grapes or refer to the colour photograph on page 51.

To make each grape take a small piece of linen, and using the appropriate colour work a single chain stitch on it. Now work trellis stitch into the outer loops of the chain stitch initially and subsequently between the bars into the row of trellis stitch above.

To ensure that your work lies flat increase as you stitch. Increases are made by working twice between the same bar occasionally. Work round and round in circles until you have covered an area of about 1 cm in diameter. When you have reached the

THREADS - COTON A BRODER 16

101	variegated green
336	dark blue
552	purple
561	dark mint green
792	violet blue
840	medium brown
gold metallic thread	

required size work a running stitch around the edge of your stitching, cut away from the fabric (there will be a little scrap under the original chain stitch) pull up into a ball, then sew to your embroidery in the correct position.

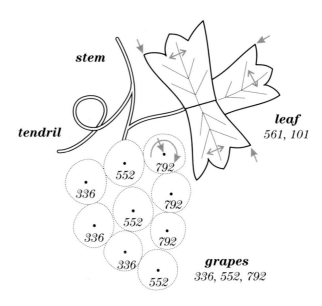

stem

tendril

leaf
561, 101

grapes
336, 552, 792

792
552
336
792
336
552
792
336
552

stems and tendril to be
chain stitched in 840

STRAWBERRY

All chain, long and short, straight, french knots and the first part of plaited stitch to be worked using a crewel No. 8 needle.

All laced chain and second part of plaited stitch to be worked using a tapestry No. 22 - 26 needle.

For best results we recommend you stitch the strawberry in the sequence given. Note the Strawberry is the only shape where the chain stitch is worked last.

STRAWBERRY FRUIT

Plaited stitch is worked to create the surface of the strawberry and this looks most attractive when it is worked over a little felt. (Plaited stitch is the only stitch I like to work in an embroidery frame.) Cut a piece of white felt the same size as the strawberry and lightly tack into place with sewing thread and a crewel No.8 needle. *Do not* work chain stitch around this shape first.

Thread your needle with 349 and bring the needle out at the *centre of the top* of the strawberry. Lay down a long thread across the centre then take the needle through to the back at the centre of the base of the strawberry.

Work satin stitch out towards one side, when completed return your needle to the centre and work satin stitch over the remaining half of the strawberry.

Using a tapestry needle, change to your second colour 677, *start at the centre on the side* of the strawberry and darn over three threads and under three to the other side. There will be odd threads at the side just keep the look of the darning correct. Work one half of the strawberry and then return to the centre and work the remaining half.

When the darning is complete work chain stitch around the strawberry in 349, this gives a nice neat outside edge to the strawberry. To enhance the strawberry, thread your needle with a gold metallic thread and make short straight stitches extending out from the strawberry. Refer to the diagram or the colour photograph on page 51 for additional detail.

THREADS - COTON A BRODER 16

349   red
367   medium green
563   light mint green
677   pale old gold
a selection of stranded cottons
gold metallic thread

SEPALS AND STEM

Outline all the sepals in chain stitch and work a straight line of chain stitch down the centre of each sepal using 563. Work the stem in chain stitch using 367 and with the same thread work the laced chain down the centre line of chain stitch on the sepals.

STRAWBERRY FLOWER

The strawberry flower is worked in long and short stitch using three threads of white stranded cotton. Cover the entire flower in long and short stitch then work a few short straight stitches using one thread of pale pink stranded cotton radiating out from the centre, these give just a faint blush of colour to the flower. The centre is worked in french knots using two threads of stranded yellow cotton.

1st row of chain ————

2nd row of chain - - - - - -

start stitching here ⟶

HANDY HINT

You may find it easier to do plait stitch on the strawberry if you start with the cream and weave with the red.

strawberry
349, 677

chain stitch is worked at the completion of the strawberry

flower

sepals
367, 563

stems

stems to be chain stitched in 367

65

Bird

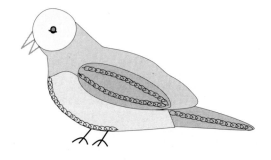

All chain, straight and ladder stitch is to be worked using a crewel No. 8 needle. All trellis and laced chain stitch to be worked using a tapestry No. 22 - 26 needle. Arrows indicate where to start stitching and the direction in which to stitch rows. For best results we recommend you stitch the bird in the sequence given.

Head
Outline in chain stitch using 973 and fill with trellis stitch worked in the same colour. Work one chain in the centre of the head and work trellis stitch around it in a spiral as you do when making a pea.

Upper Body
Outline in chain stitch using 740 and fill with trellis stitch worked in the same colour. *Start by the head, where indicated.* This is worked all over the upper body area, including where the wing will subsequently be worked. Whilst you have the correct thread in your needle stitch the beak in four short straight stitches, refer to the diagram.

Breast
This area is worked in two rows of ladder stitch using 211 which gives the 'feel' of feathers sweeping back. To give added plumpness to the breast an additional row of chain stitch has been worked. Refer to the coloured photograph on page 51 for additonal detail.

Wing
To create a more feathery appearance, the wing has been worked in laced chain using 349. Stitch two rows of chain stitch down the upper body area on top of the trellis stitch which has already been worked here, refer to the diagram for details. Next work the lacing into the chain stitch.

THREADS - COTON A BRODER 16
211   mauve
349   red
740   orange
792   violet blue
973   hard yellow
black stranded cotton

TAIL

The tail feathers are also worked in laced chain. Outline the tail section in chain stitch using 792. Work one row of chain stitch down the centre of this area and then work the lacing into the centre row of chain stitch.

The bird is completed by stitching a small bead to the head for the eye and stitching the legs and feet using black stranded cotton.

There is no padding required on the bird.

shape edge ....
1st row of chain ─────
2nd row of chain ─ ─ ─ ─
3rd row of chain ·············

start stitching here ⟶
direction of rows ⟷

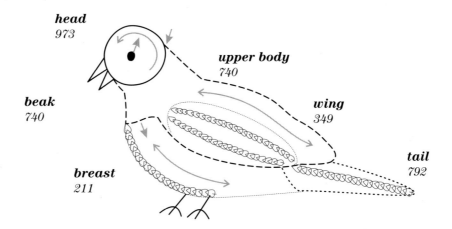

head
973

upper body
740

beak
740

wing
349

breast
211

tail
792

ACORNS

All chain and stem stitch to be worked using a crewel No. 8 needle.

All detached buttonhole and trellis stitch to be worked using a tapestry No. 22 - 26 needle.

Arrows indicate where to start stitching and the direction in which to stitch rows. For best results we recommend you stitch the acorns in the sequence given.

STEMS

Work in chain stitch using 301.

CUPULE

Outline in chain stitch then fill with trellis stitch using 301 throughout.

NUT

Outline in chain stitch with 3032. Fill the area with detached buttonhole stitch worked using 3032 and bronze coloured metallic thread in the needle together and worked as one.

LEAF

Outline in chain stitch, then fill with detached buttonhole stitch worked using 469 and multi-coloured metallic thread in the needle together worked as one, to cover the entire leaf area. Work the vein markings in stem stitch using 301. Refer to the colour photograph on page 51 for additional detail. The use of metallic threads is entirely optional but it does give that added sparkle to your embroidery!

1st row of chain ──────

2nd row of chain - - - - - -

start stitching here ⟶

direction of rows ⟷

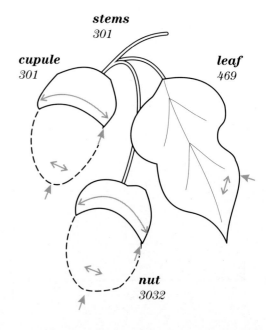

stems
301

cupule
301

leaf
469

nut
3032

THREADS - COTON A BRODER 16

301   rust

469   olive green

3032   taupe

bronze and multi-coloured metallic thread

PEAR

All chain, straight and stem stitch to be worked using a crewel No. 8 needle. All detached buttonhole stitch to be worked using a tapestry No. 22-26 needle. Arrows indicate where to start stitching and the direction in which to stitch rows. For best results we recommend you stitch the pear in the sequence given.

STEM AND LEAF

Using 471 work the stem and leaf outline in chain stitch. Still using 471 *start at the upper point* of the leaf and fill with detached buttonhole stitch. Pad a little and close. Work the vein in stem stitch using 469.

PEAR

Outline in chain stitch using 3782. Note the angle the pear is stitched in to create the interesting line of the colour change. Work in detached buttonhole stitch *starting at the top* with 369, then change to 471 for the middle section and finally to 3782 refer to the diagram or colour photograph on page 51 for additional detail. When using 369 and 471 combine them with bronze metallic thread and stitch the two threads together in the needle as one. Pad a little and close.

Using the bronze metallic thread stitch three straight stitches up from the base of the pear as shown in the diagram.

THREADS - COTON A BRODER 16
369 light green
469 olive green
471 light olive green
3782 fawn
bronze metallic thread

colour change
1st row of chain

start stitching here
direction of rows

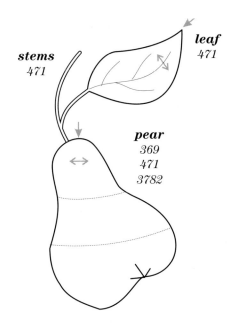

stems 471
leaf 471
pear 369 471 3782

CATERPILLARS

PLAIN CATERPILLAR

THREADS - COTON A BRODER 16
727   citrus yellow
801   dark brown
945   peach

All chain and stem stitches to be worked using a crewel No. 8 needle.

Work two rows of chain stitch side by side using 801 for one row and 945 for the other, following the curve drawn for your caterpillar. Outline in stem stitch using 727.

caterpillar
801, 945, 727

SEGMENTED CATERPILLAR

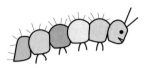

THREADS - COTON A BRODER 16
552   purple
553   medium purple
743   yellow
782   mustard
793   light violet blue
840   medium brown
green stranded cotton
multi-coloured metallic thread

All chain, satin and straight stitch is to be worked using a crewel No. 8 needle. All detached buttonhole stitch to be worked using a tapestry No. 22 - 26 needle.

Arrows indicate where to start stitching and the direction in which to stitch rows. For best results we recommend you stitch the caterpillar in the sequence given. Outline all the segments (not the head) of the caterpillar in chain stitch using 552. Each of the segments of the

caterpillar is filled with detached buttonhole stitch worked in the colours indicated on the diagram below or refer to the colour photograph on page 51 for additional detail. Pad each section in the usual manner before closing.

The head is worked in satin stitch using a scrap of medium green stranded cotton. The feelers, eyes, mouth and feet have been worked in small straight stitches using 840. The fine hairs on the back of the caterpillar have been worked in small straight stitches using multi-coloured metallic thread.

1st row of chain ────────

start stitching here ───→
direction of rows ←──→

caterpillar
552

793   552   782   743
553

SNAIL

THREADS - COTON A BRODER 16
224   medium Paris pink
815   ruby red
945   peach
3032   taupe
silver metallic thread

All chain, straight and stem stitch is to be worked using a crewel No. 8 needle. All trellis and detached buttonhole stitch to be worked using a tapestry No. 22 - 26 needle.

Arrows indicate where to start stitching and the direction in which to stitch rows. For best results we recommend you stitch the snail in the sequence given.

SNAIL BODY

Outline the body of the snail in chain stitch worked in 3032. It is filled by working trellis stitch with two different threads to give added interest to the shape. *Start stitching along the lower edge* of the snail using 3032, work trellis stitch for two rows then change to 815 and work two to three more rows to finish the body. Pad a little before closing.

SNAIL SHELL

The snail shell and the divisions within the shell are outlined in chain stitch using 945. The areas within the shell are filled in detached buttonhole stitch. Refer to the diagram for the colours worked in the different sections of the snail or refer to the colour photograph on page 51. *Do not* pad the sections of the snail shell.
On completion of the snail shell separate the different sections of the shell with silver metallic thread and long straight stitches. Work the feelers in stem stitch using silver metallic thread and sew a little silver bead at the end of each feeler.

HANDY HINT
I worked the snail shell with two needles - 224 in one needle and 945 in the other and changed over for each segment.

colour change	....
1st row of chain	——————
2nd row of chain	- - - - - -
start stitching here	→
direction of rows	↔

shell outline
945

945   945

224   224

224

945

224

body
3032, 815

BUTTERFLY

THREADS - COTON A BRODER 16
602   raspberry pink
742   dark yellow
930   slate blue
multi-coloured metallic thread
oddments of stranded cotton

All chain, straight and satin stitch is to be worked using a crewel No. 8 needle. All detached buttonhole and trellis stitch to be worked using a tapestry No. 22 - 26 needle.

Arrows indicate where to start stitching and the direction in which to stitch rows. For best results we recommend you stitch the butterfly in the sequence given.

INSECT BODY

Outline the thorax (central area) and abdomen of the butterfly's body in chain stitch using 742.

Still using 742 fill the thorax using detached buttonhole stitch, pad a little before closing. Refer to the diagram for angle of working and where to start.

The abdomen is worked in trellis stitch. Start with two rows of 602 then work two rows using 742, two more of 602, with the balance stitched using 742. Pad a little before closing. Refer to the diagram for the colours used or refer to the colour photograph on page 51 for additonal detail.

WINGS

Both wings are outlined in chain stitch using 930. The wings are filled with detached buttonhole stitch using 930 and multi-coloured metallic thread in the needle together and stitched as one.

Refer to the diagram to see where to start stitching each wing. Do not pad the wings.

The butterfly's head is worked in satin stitch using light green stranded cotton. The feelers, feet and an eye are stitched in straight stitch using one thread of brown stranded cotton.

colour change	·········
1st row of chain	———
2nd row of chain	- - - -
start stitching here	→
direction of rows	↔

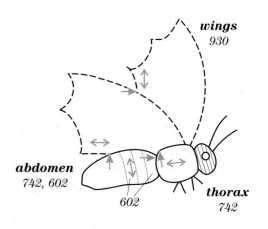

FOUR OUTER LEAVES

All chain and stem stitch is to be worked using a crewel No. 8 needle.

All detached buttonhole stitch to be worked using a tapestry No. 22 - 26 needle.

Arrows indicate where to start stitching and the direction in which to stitch rows.

LEAVES

Work the stems and outline the leaves in chain stitch using 904 then fill with detached buttonhole stitch worked using 101 to cover entire leaf area. Work the vein markings in stem stitch using bronze metallic thread. Refer to the colour photograph on page 51 for additional detail.

1st row of chain

start stitching here
direction of rows

stems
904

leaves
904, 101

THREADS - COTON A BRODER 16

101   variegated green
904   apple green
bronze metallic thread

73

The Sampler

The Sampler is a beautiful introduction to the many different flowers, insects, bird and leaves used throughout this book. By stitching the sampler you will learn the various stitches and the different techniques commonly used in this embroidery. We have framed the Sampler but it would make a most attractive cushion and in Elizabethan times this was a very popular use for the embroidery.

The Sampler pattern on pages 76 - 77 gives the outlines of all the flowers etc used in this book. The Sampler pattern gives *only the lines to be traced* and omits finer details that might not be covered with the final stitching.

Detailed instructions on how to stitch each of the flowers, insects, bird and leaves are given in the shapes section, including the needles, threads and stitches used to stitch the entire shape. The coloured photograph on page 51 may be referred to for additional detail.

Samplers were originally stitched as a learning exercise and reference for their owners. This sampler is no exception.

The ogee outline, tendrils and small branches are all stitched using a medium brown thread. The tendrils fill up the odd spaces and are important as they help to create the 'busy' effect desired in this type of embroidery. This stitching provides the framework for the flowers and leaves and the muted brown enhances the colourful threads to be used in the flowers.

The Elizabethan embroiderer used gilt thread and jewels freely to enrich her embroidery. I have also used silver and gold threads as well as taking advantage of the rayon metallic threads available to the modern embroiderer. I have replaced the use of precious jewels with beads, sequins and diamantes and their addition gives this embroidery added sparkle.

All chain and stem stitch to be worked using a Crewel No. 8 needle. It will be easier to do the whipping if you change to a Tapestry No. 22 - 26 needle.

THREADS - COTON A BRODER 16
840   medium brown
gold metallic thread

Trace the Sampler on to a piece of closely woven linen 40 x 50cm, (see how to transfer the design on page 13). The sampler is spread over two pages, make sure you match the design exactly on the centre lines. You may find it easier to trace the design first to a large sheet of paper and then to your fabric. Remember to apply interlining before you start to stitch.

The entire ogee outline is stitched first with one row of chain stitch and one row of stem stitch worked side by side, then whip one side of the chain stitch and the stem stitch with gold metallic thread to create a cord like effect.

Next embroider each flower etc, following the instructions given in the shapes section pages 34 - 73.

Block when complete, see page 14 for instructions on blocking.

DIAGRAM OF THE COMPLETE SAMPLER PATTERN

GUIDELINES FOR TRACING THE SAMPLER DESIGN *(see overleaf)*
Strong dotted lines indicate where the pattern joins. Centre the design on the fabric.
Trace only the solid lines. Fine dotted lines indicate outside edge of placed objects
Solid dots indicate the centre point for the placement of objects such as grapes, beads etc.

TOP

centering line

TOP

centering line

77

Pin Cushions

PIN CUSHION PATTERN - ACORN

These pin cushions were inspired by the 'undress' hats that were worn at home in the evening by the well-dressed man of the sixteenth to seventeenth century when he removed his wig.

The original 'undress' hats were heavily embroidered with flowers and embellished with beads and gilt thread. The charm of the early hats is recaptured in these delightful pin cushions which are somewhat quicker to stitch than their earlier counterparts!

Three different designs are given. Our examples have been worked on furnishing remnants 15 x 30 cm in size which we then stabilised with iron-on interlining, but any closely woven linen would be satisfactory. The pear and strawberrry pin cushions are quicker to embroider than the pin cushion featuring the acorn design.

Trace the outline of the pin cushion on to your fabric, a seam allowance is included, and then trace the motif you wish to use. Notes on how to transfer the design to your fabric are given on page 13. The pattern is given for the pear, to create a pattern for the strawberry pin cushion trace the outline first, then the strawberry and flower motifs. Likewise, create a pattern for the acorn pin cushion by repeating the acorn and leaf motif, shown at the top of this page, in each of the curved sections. *Do not* cut out the pin cushion until your embroidery is complete. Stitch the design using the threads and following the instructions for the acorn and leaf given on page 68, the pear given on page 69, or the strawberry and flower given on page 64 of the shape section.

When you have completed the embroidery apply the cord and beads, if used, to the material then block if necessary. Now cut out the pin cushion, (the notch at the centre of each curve shows where to finish each seam and where to place the tassel). Place the tassel and sew the seams together. Fill with stuffing then cut a flat piece of stiff cardboard 6 cm in diameter and lace fabric over it (you will need an 8 cm circle of fabric) or use heavy iron on vilene to stiffen your base then sew to the bottom of the pin cushion. Your pin cushion is now complete.

PIN CUSHION PATTERN -STRAWBERRY

Place a strawberry then a flower alternately in the centre of each curved section of the pincushion.

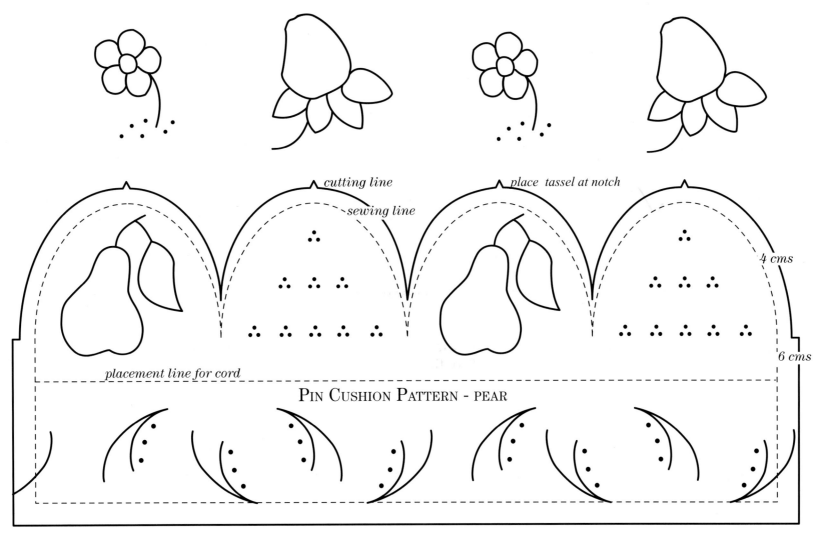

cutting line

sewing line

place tassel at notch

4 cms

6 cms

placement line for cord

PIN CUSHION PATTERN - PEAR

'SWETE BAGE'

This lovely evening bag is worked very much
in the style of the 'swete bages' of the
late sixteenth and early seventeenth centuries.

The original bags were worn suspended from the waist and frequently had a tiny pin cushion hanging from one corner. They were usually decorated with tassels attached along the lower edge of the bag and hanging from the drawstrings. They may also have been filled with sweet smelling herbs and placed amongst clothes and linen when stored. Our bag features the heavy scrolling so popular in the original embroidery and the lovely foxglove and pomegranate flowers. The handmade cord and tassels used on our bag are a continuation in the rich tradition of embroiderers through the centuries.

Trace the 'Swete Bage' pattern and embroidery design given on pages 82 - 83 on to a large sheet of paper first and then to your fabric. The pattern is spread over two pages, make sure you match the design exactly on the centre lines.

We made this bag on a piece of closely woven linen 70 cm wide x 40 cm long. Position the pattern for the bag about 5 cm in from the bottom and one side of the material and about 8 cm from the top. *Do not cut out the bag at this stage.* Transfer the design on to your fabric, see how to transfer the design on page 13. Keep the paper pattern to one side as you will need to re-use this when your embroidery is completed and it is time to cut out the bag.

The foxglove flowers have been worked with the same colours, except for one, that were used on the Sampler but we have used a different selection of threads for the pomegranate flowers. Remember to iron on interlining to strengthen the fabric before you start to stitch.

Refer to the colour photograph of
the 'Swete Bage' on
page 53 for additional detail

SCROLLING

THREADS - COTON A BRODER 16
840   medium brown
3328   coral

The scrolling is worked in
ladder stitch using 840. To
enhance it, little straight
stitches have been worked
on each side of the line of stitching in
groups of three, 5 mms apart, using 3328.

FOXGLOVES AND LEAVES

These are all worked in the one colour
range and are stitched with
the colours used in the
Sampler with one
exception, the calyx is
filled with light olive
green, 471 not brown. Refer
to the foxglove flower in the
shape section on page 34
for instructions on stitching
these flowers.

POMEGRANATE

The two pomegranates have each been
stitched with a different thread selection
but they have been worked using the
same stitches as were used in the
Sampler.
Detailed instructions for stitching the
pomegranate are on page 60.

The colours used to stitch the left hand
pomegranate are as follows.

THREADS - COTON A BRODER 16
336   dark blue
469   light olive
       green
797   royal blue
799   medium blue
800   light blue
multi-coloured metallic
thread

Outline the calyx in chain stitch using
469. Fill the area with detached
buttonhole stitch worked using 469 and
multi-coloured metallic thread in the
needle together and worked as one. Pad
a little and close.
The seed is outlined in chain stitch and
filled with trellis stitch using 800.

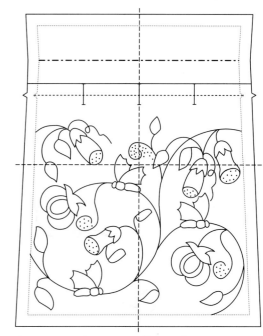

*Diagram of complete 'Swete Bage' pattern
with seam allowances added*

PATTERN INSTRUCTIONS

*Strong dotted lines indicate where the
pattern joins.
Trace only the solid lines.
Solid dots indicate the centre point for the
placement of beads.
Position the pattern for the bag 5 cms in
from the bottom and one side of fabric and
8 cm down from the top. DO NOT cut out
the bag shape until after the design has
been worked.*

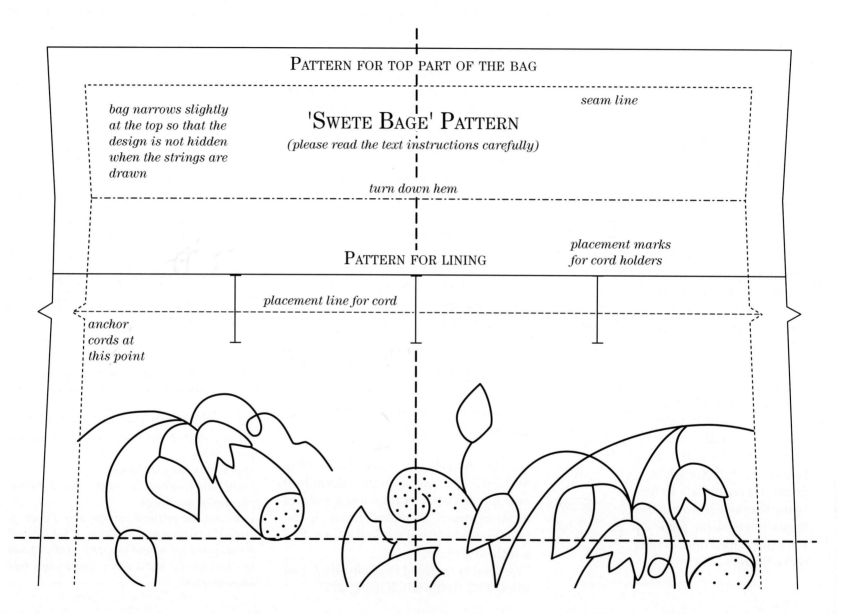

PATTERN FOR TOP PART OF THE BAG

'SWETE BAGE' PATTERN

(please read the text instructions carefully)

seam line

*bag narrows slightly
at the top so that the
design is not hidden
when the strings are
drawn*

turn down hem

PATTERN FOR LINING

*placement marks
for cord holders*

placement line for cord

*anchor
cords at
this point*

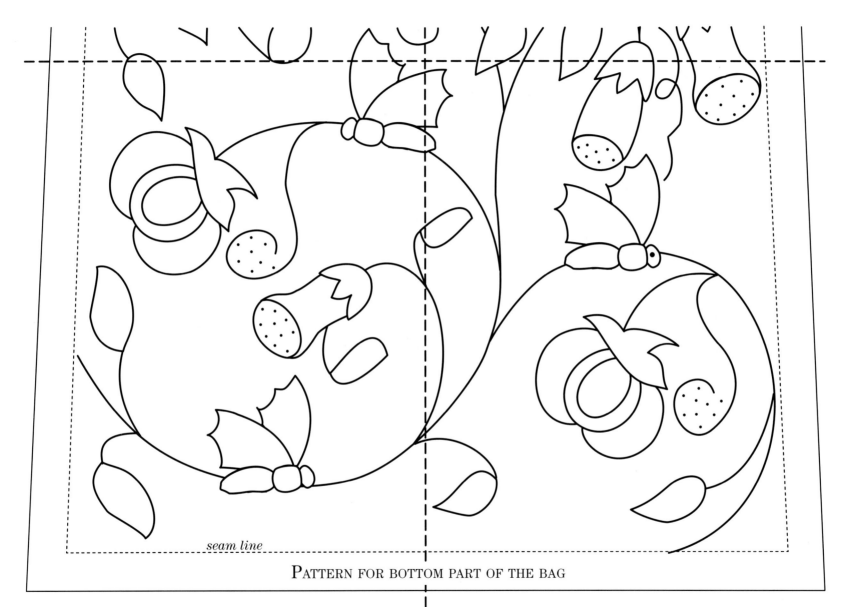

seam line

PATTERN FOR BOTTOM PART OF THE BAG

Refer to the colour photograph of
the 'Swete Bage' on
page 53 for additional detail

The curved line outlining the 'flesh' of
the pomegranate is worked in chain
stitch using 336 and filled with trellis
stitch using 797.

The outer line, or skin, is worked in
chain stitch using 797 and filled with
trellis stitch using 799 with a stripe of
797.

The colours used to stitch the right hand
pomegranate are as follows.

THREADS - COTON A BRODER 16
504   light sea green
561   dark mint green
792   violet blue
793   light violet blue
multi-coloured metallic thread

Outline the calyx in chain stitch using
561. Fill the area with detached
buttonhole stitch worked using 561 and
multi-coloured metallic thread in the
needle together and worked as one. Pad
a little and close.

The seed is outlined in chain stitch and
filled with trellis stitch using 504.

The curved line outlining the 'flesh' of
the pomegranate is worked in chain
stitch using 561 and filled with trellis
stitch using 792.

The outer line, or skin, is worked in
chain stitch using 792 and filled with
trellis stitch using 793 with a stripe of
792.

BUTTERFLIES

All worked in the same way. Full
instructions for working the butterfly
are given on page 72.

THREADS - COTON
A BRODER 16
336   dark blue
727   citrus yellow
930   dark steel blue
3328   coral
fawn and dark brown stranded cotton
silver and multi-coloured metallic thread.

Outline the thorax (central area) and
fill with detached buttonhole stitch
using 727.
Outline the abdomen with 727 fill with
trellis stitch using 727 but working two
stripes of 3328 at the top of the abdomen.

Both wings are outlined in chain stitch
with 336 and filled with detached
buttonhole stitch using 930 and multi-
coloured metallic thread in the needle
together and stitched as one. The circles
on the wings are worked in silver metallic
thread in spider web stitch.

The head is worked in satin stitch using
two threads of fawn stranded cotton.

Work feelers, feet and eye in straight
stitch using one thread of stranded dark
brown cotton.

To add the final touch to your embroidery
sew some light blue glass beads above
the top butterfly and some darker blue
beads by the pomegranates as shown in
the colour photograph on page 53. Block
when complete, for instructions on
blocking see page 14.

TO MAKE BAG

finished bag approximately 19 x 22.5 cm

Before you begin to make your bag, make the cord and tassels as these are sewn into the bag during its construction.

TO MAKE CORD AND TASSELS

1 skein No. 5 Perle 822 Ivory, 224 medium Paris pink and 369 light green.
Cut 5 lengths of 822 x 1.4 m in length
Cut 1 length of 224 x 1.4 m in length
Cut 1 length of 369 x 1.4 m in length
Twist all together to make cord.

Cover two curtain rings 1.5 cm in diameter with buttonhole stitch using 822 and make 2 tassels using 224 that will slip through the finished curtain rings, leave to one side.

With your embroidery completed and blocked it is now time to cut out the 'Swete Bage' shape using the pattern you traced before you started to stitch. Cut out the front carefully, positioning the pattern piece on top of your embroidery, then cut the back out of the remaining fabric - it is plain.

Cut out lining fabric (it is shorter than the outside fabric see line marked on the pattern).

Mark with pins where the loops to thread the cord are to be worked. These are stitched in buttonhole stitch on the right side, over four threads using No. 5 Perle 822.

Before sewing the side seams of the bag I thread the twisted cord through the loops on both sides of the bag threading on rings and tassels before I machine cord the ends into one side of the bag, (note where this is marked on the pattern). This gets rid of the knots at the ends of the cord very neatly and tidily. Now with right sides of the bag together sew side seams and bottom edge.

Sew lining side seams only. Leave the bottom edge OPEN. Press all seams open.
Place lining and main bag right sides together and sew TOP EDGE.

Fold over outside fabric on fold line, press. Pin down hem. Now lift lining up so that you can herringbone top seam edge to inside of bag (making

sure your stitches don't show on the outside) this will keep your fold line neat. Close bottom edge of lining by turning in raw edges and hand stitching a small seam along the edge.

Push lining back inside bag. Push out corners. Finish with three more tassels along the base of the bag. (These tassels are threaded through covered rings 1 cm in diameter.) Well done! Your bag is complete.

HANDY HINT
To make your tassels fluffy steam them by holding above a boiling kettle, then trim the ends to neaten.

THE CAT

Cats have a charm all of their own and what could be more appealing than this feline beauty richly embroidered in a variety of flowers.

To create this delightful and very different cat, begin by tracing the design in the usual manner on to a piece of closely woven linen 35 x 45 cm. Refer to page 13 for notes on how to transfer the design. Centre the design on your fabric as this makes it easier for the framer later on.

We have used different colours for some of the flowers used in embroidering the cat, but they have been stitched in the *same manner* as described in the shape section for the relevant flower. *Check the special instructions given here for stitching each flower* before referring to the detailed instructions given in the shape section. Remember to iron on interlining before you start to stitch.

Stitch the outline of the cat, its legs, paws and tail markings last. There are no lifted up petals on the flowers in this embroidery.

Position the cat in the centre of your fabric leaving a generous amount extending beyond the design for framing

Trace the design with a very fine tipped pen or pencil to ensure that all markings are subsequently covered by your stitches

Solid dots indicate placement of beads

Refer to the colour photograph
of 'the Cat' on
page 54 for additional detail

BLOSSOM

- do not work lifted up petals.
Full instructions for
working the
blossom are
given on
page 42.

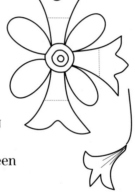

THREADS - COTON A BRODER 16
223   Paris pink
224   medium Paris pink
225   light Paris pink
469   olive green

Outline centre in chain stitch with 469 and complete with a coloured diamante.
Outline and fill petals with detached buttonhole stitch using 225, 224 and 223. See above diagram for the use of threads.

The extensions between the blossom petals have been chain stitched in 469 with a little white pearl sewn at the end of each extension.

HONEYSUCKLE

Full instructions
for working the
honeysuckle are
given on page 50.

THREADS - COTON
A BRODER 16
367   medium green
369   light green
758   salmon
948   palest peach
silver metallic thread

Outline centre in chain stitch with 758 complete with a sequin.
Outline petals in chain stitch with 948 and fill with detached buttonhole stitch starting with 948 and changing to 758 where indicated.
Chain stitch seed outline in 367 and fill with detached buttonhole stitch using 369.

Chain stitch bud outline and fill with detached buttonhole stitch using 758 throughout. Three straight stitches have been worked in silver metallic thread to complete the bud.

To highlight the honeysuckle sew a sprinkling of beads where indicated below and around the lower petal.

PRIMROSE FLOWERS

Two on the head and one on the right leg.
These have been stitched using the same colours as were used on the Sampler.
Full instructions for working the primrose flowers are given on page 38.

PANSY BUD ON TAIL

Full instructions for working the pansy bud are given on page 44.

THREADS - COTON A BRODER 16
367   medium green
727   citrus yellow
743   yellow

Calyx outline in chain stitch and fill with detached buttonhole stitch using 367 throughout.

Outline bud in chain stitch using 727 and fill with detached buttonhole stitch using 743 for the first two rows and 727 for the balance.

CONVOLVULUS

- do not work lifted up petals.
Full instructions for working the convolvulus are given on page 46.

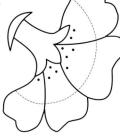

THREADS - COTON A BRODER 16
561   dark mint green
800   light blue
931   steel blue
oddments of olive green stranded cotton

The receptacle is worked in satin stitch using two threads of olive green stranded cotton.
Outline calyx in chain stitch and fill with detached buttonhole stitch using 561.
Outline petals in chain stitch using 800, still using 800 starting at the outer edge of the petal work detached buttonhole

stitch to cover half the petal area then change to 931 to complete.
Sew a few dark blue glass beads where indicated to further enhance the convolvulus.

CATERPILLAR

The caterpillar has been stitched using the same threads as the Sampler except that its face has been worked in bright green stranded cotton. Full instructions for working the caterpillar are given on page 70.

BIG BUDS

WITH BEADS AND EXTENSIONS
ON CAT'S BODY

Full instructions for working the buds are given on page 42.

THREADS - COTON A BRODER 16
224   medium Paris pink

Outline in chain stitch and fill with detached buttonhole stitch using 224 throughout.
With the same thread sew three straight stitches out from the tip of each bud

and sew a little white pearl at the end of each stitch.

SEED PODS ON THE LEGS

These are worked in satin stitch using oddments of pink stranded cotton.

PEA POD

- do not work lifted up flap or individual peas.
Full instructions for working the pea pod are given on page 48.

THREADS - COTON A BRODER 16
101   variegated green
504   light sea green
561   dark mint green

Outline the leaves in chain stitch and work one row of chain stitch down the middle of each leaf using 561.
Next outline the pea pod in chain stitch and fill with detached buttonhole stitch worked using 101 throughout.

With the rest of the pea pod completed now work the lacing down the central line of chain stitch on each leaf using 504.

ALL OTHER LEAVES

These are all worked in the same way.

THREADS - COTON A BRODER 16
101   variegated green
silver metallic thread

Outline and fill with detached button-hole stitched using 101. The vein markings have been worked in stem stitch using silver metallic thread.

FACE MARKINGS

The face markings outlining the eyes, down past the nose and round the mouth are worked in *back stitch* using *two* threads of stranded cotton DMC 3740.

The three lines on the forehead and the line up into the left ear are worked in *stem stitch* using *two* threads of DMC 3740 stranded cotton.

The centre of the nose and the pupils of the eyes are worked in *satin stitch* using *three* threads of DMC3740 stranded cotton. The tongue and eyes are worked in satin stitch using oddments of pink and fawn stranded cotton respectively.

All the tendrils and stems are worked in *chain stitch* using *two* threads of DMC 3740 stranded cotton.

Do *not* stitch the outlines yet.

TO MAKE UP

When you have embroidered the flowers on the cat, block your embroidery. Refer to page 14 for instructions on blocking. Now tack the embroidery to a second piece of fabric e.g. pre-washed calico. I then machined the two layers together marking in the outlines using my zipper foot. The outline of the cat, its face, divisions for feet, paws and tail are shown by a double line in the diagram on page 86. Next I embroidered over my machined outline in *chain stitch* using *two* threads of DMC 3042 stranded cotton.

To give the cat its three dimensional appearance I slashed the calico attached to the back of the cat and inserted a little padding. I found that a short fat knitting needle or crochet hook were the best tools for stuffing. I started with the paws which were tricky! I then did the tail, legs, body and head. Make numerous small cuts to insert the padding rather than just a few big slashes. Catch the fabric back together and your embroidery is now ready to be taken to your favourite framer!

We have used the pansy flower but any of the flowers with the more rounded edges would be suitable.

To make the serviette rings using the pansy you will need a piece of closely woven linen 20 cm square. Trace the pansy four times from the sampler pattern (see page 13 for notes on how to transfer the design) and embroider following the instructions given in the shape section on page 44. Remember to iron on interlining before you start to stitch. Block, see page 14, when complete.

TO MAKE UP

Cut round the pansies leaving about 6 mm of fabric extending beyond the embroidery, cut into the flower at regular intervals then fold the fabric to the back of the pansy, hold in place with fabric glue or stitch.

When dry draw round the outside of the pansy and cut out another piece of fabric exactly the same shape as the pansy, glue to the back, the glue will stop the edges fraying.

Now make twelve rouleaus, four each of yellow, mauve and purple. (Cut the rouleaus on the cross grain of the fabric about 2 cm wide by 25 cm in length.) To enable you to shape the rings nicely, insert florist wire into the rouleaus and plait one each of the yellow, mauve and purple rouleaus together. To complete your serviette ring sew each end of the plait to the back of a pansy. Your serviette ring is now complete. Repeat this for each of the three remaining pansies.

An attractive table setting helps create the right atmosphere of anticipation and enthusiasm for a delicious meal. These lovely pansy serviette rings will help set the scene for any meal.

WOODLAND NYMPH

Sprites and fairies were very much part of the Elizabethan environment and were frequently referred to in literature of the period. This woodland nymph has a much more twentieth century look to her!

The face is easily embroidered using one thread of stranded cotton and is stitched using satin, stem and back stitches. We used toning, random-dyed, stranded cotton for the eyebrows and circle underneath, olive green for the eyes, a deep pink for the mouth and soft brown for the outline of the face and neck. Trace the face and neck *using a soft lead pencil*, on to a piece of closely woven linen about 35 x 45cm, centre the design. Trace the rest of the design with your usual marker. Remember to apply interlining before you start to stitch.

The woodland nymph is stitched using different colours for the flowers through-out but they have been stitched in the same manner as described in the shape section for the relevant flower. *Check the special instructions given here for each flower* before referring to the detailed instructions given in the shape section.

WOODLAND NYMPH PATTERN

Draw the face and neck in pencil and the rest of the design with your usual marker. Solid dots indicate placement for beads.

Position face in the centre of the fabric with a minimum of 10 cm of fabric extending beyond the design in all directions.

Refer to the colour photograph of the 'Woodland Nymph' on page 55 for additional detail

TENDRILS

THREADS - COTON A BRODER 16
3032 taupe

The tendrils are stitched using 3032 throughout. Work chain and stem stitch together in the wider areas, just use stem stitch towards the tips.

PEAR AND PEAR LEAF

Full instructions for working the pear are given on page 69.

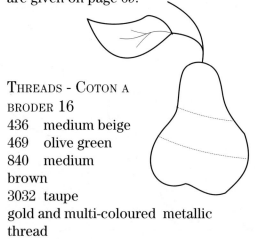

THREADS - COTON A BRODER 16
436 medium beige
469 olive green
840 medium brown
3032 taupe
gold and multi-coloured metallic thread

Stitch the stem and outline the pear in chain stitch worked using 3032. Starting at the top and still using 3032 work in detached buttonhole stitch to cover about a third of the area, then change to 436 for the middle area and 840 for the base. When using 840 combine it with multi-coloured metallic thread and stitch the two threads together in the needle as one. Work the entire pear, the cornflower is worked over the top of the pear.

Outline the pear leaf in chain stitch and fill with detached buttonhole stitch worked using 469 throughout. Work the veins in stem stitch using gold metallic thread.

BLOSSOM

Full instructions for working the blossom are given on page 42.

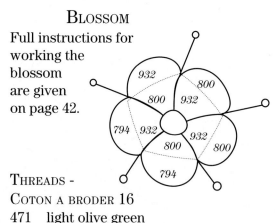

THREADS -
COTON A BRODER 16
471 light olive green
727 citrus yellow

794 cornflower blue
800 light blue
932 grey blue
gold metallic thread

Outline the centre in chain stitch with 727 and sew a diamante in the centre to complete.

Outline and fill petals with detached buttonhole stitch using 932, 794 and 800, refer to the diagram for their use.

The lifted up petals are stitched in the same variations of thread as the petals beneath. To complete they are edged in buttonhole stitch using gold metallic thread.

Embroider the lines extending from between each petal of the blossom in chain stitch using 471. Sew a little white pearl bead at the end of each extension.

LEAVES

Full instructions for working these leaves are given on page 73.

THREADS - COTON A BRODER 16
502 medium sea green
504 light sea green
561 dark mint green
gold and bronze metallic thread

THREE LEAVES ACROSS TOP OF HEAD

For the left and right hand top leaves chain stitch the outlines using 561. To create a nice shadowed effect fill with detached buttonhole stitch, start using 561 but change half way to 502. Outline the central top leaf in chain stitch and fill with detached buttonhole stitch using 561.

THE LARGE LEAF ON THE LEFT BELOW THE CORNFLOWER

Outline in chain stitch and filled with detached buttonhole stitch using 502.
Vein markings are worked on all the above leaves in stem stitch using bronze metallic thread.

THE LARGE LEAF ON THE RIGHT HAND SIDE OF THE FACE

Outline in chain stitch using 502, fill with detached buttonhole stitch, start using 502 but change to 504 half way down.

Vein markings are worked on this leaf in gold metallic thread.

CORNFLOWER

Full instructions for working the cornflower are given on page 36.

THREADS - COTON A BRODER 16
469   olive green
677   pale old gold
754   soft pink
3328 coral

Outline the calyx in chain stitch and fill with detached buttonhole stitch worked using 469.
The petals are outlined in chain stitch using 677, the top one is worked over the top of the pear.
Work in detached buttonhole stitch filling each petal with three bands of colour changing from 677 at the outer edge to 754 in the middle and 3328 in the centre. Do *not* pad. When complete, sew some beads where shown to enhance your embroidery.

ACORNS

Full instructions for working the acorns are given on page 68.

THREADS - COTON A BRODER 16
471   light olive green
3032 taupe
bronze metallic thread

Outline the cupule in chain stitch then fill with trellis stitch using 3032 throughout. The nut is outlined in chain stitch using 471. Fill the area with detached buttonhole stitch worked using 471 and bronze coloured metallic thread in the needle together and worked as one.

LARGE BUD

LOWER LEFT HAND SIDE OF FACE

Full instructions for working the bud are given on page 42.

THREADS - COTON A BRODER 16
793   light violet blue

Outline in chain stitch and fill with detached buttonhole stitch

Refer to the colour photograph of the 'Woodland Nymph' on page 55 for additional detail

worked using 793. Work three small straight stitches out from the end of the bud and sew a pearl at the end of each stitch.

FOXGLOVES

Full instructions for working the foxglove are given on page 34.

THREADS - COTON A BRODER 16
504 light sea green
742 dark yellow
743 yellow
840 medium brown
945 peach
multi-coloured metallic thread

Both flowers are worked in the same way.

Outline the calyx in chain stitch using 840 and fill with detached buttonhole stitch worked using 840 and multi-coloured metallic thread in the needle together worked as one.

Chain stitch round the main part of each flower using 743. Then work in trellis stitch filling the area with three bands of colour starting at the outer edge with 743 then changing to 945 and finally to 742.

Outline the outer lip in chain stitch and fill with detached buttonhole using 504.

To complete the foxglove sew some small bronze bugle beads here to add a sparkle!

PRIMROSE FLOWERS

YELLOW SINGLE PRIMROSE AT TOP AND MAUVE PRIMROSE FLOWERS

Full instructions for working the primrose are given on page 38.

THREADS - COTON A BRODER 16
211 mauve
301 rust

407 mushroom brown
727 citrus yellow
792 violet blue
793 light violet blue
3032 taupe

To stitch the yellow primrose, outline each petal in chain stitch and fill with detached buttonhole stitch worked using 727. The centre has been highlighted with a small yellow bead. The stem up to it is chain stitched using 3032.

To stitch the mauve primroses outline the flower centres in chain stitch using 301 and complete with a sequin sewn in the centre.

Outline the petals in chain stitch using the colour to match subsequent stitching. Sew the petals in detached buttonhole stitch using 792, 793 and 211. Refer to the colour photograph on page 55 for the threads to be used for each petal.

To stitch the floral tubes work chain stitch around shape and in a straight line down the centres using 407. Work laced chain down the centre line of chain stitch using 301.

LITTLE LEAF
ADJACENT TO RIGHT CHEEK

Full instructions for working this leaf are in the daffodil section and are given on page 40.

THREADS - COTON A BRODER 16
469   olive green
gold metallic thread

Outline and fill with detached button-hole stitch using 469 throughout. Work vein markings in stem stitch using gold metallic thread.

HONEYSUCKLE BUDS
ON FOREHEAD AND LOWER RIGHT HAND SIDE OF FACE

Full instructions for working the honeysuckle bud are given on page 50.

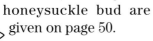

THREADS - COTON A BRODER 16
677 pale old gold
792 violet blue
3328   coral
3032   taupe
gold metallic thread

All buds are outlined in chain stitch and filled with detached buttonhole stitch. The bud on the forehead is worked using 792 throughout.

The stems down to the two lower buds are worked in chain stitch using 3032. The bud below the butterfly is stitched using 677 throughout and the bud at the neckline is stitched using 3328 throughout.

Three straight stitches have been worked in gold metallic thread on all the buds.

BUTTERFLY

Full instructions for working the butterfly are given on page 72.

THREADS - COTON
A BRODER 16
563   light mint green
754   soft pink
3328 coral
multi-coloured metallic thread
oddments of yellow and black stranded cotton.

Outline the thorax (central area) and abdomen of the butterfly's body in chain stitch using 3328.

Still using 3328 fill the thorax using detached buttonhole stitch.

The abdomen is filled using trellis stitch worked using 3328 with two stripes of 563 at the top of the abdomen.

Both wings are outlined in chain stitch using 754 and filled with detached buttonhole stitch still using 754 plus multi-coloured metallic thread in the needle and stitched as one.

The butterfly is finished with the head worked in satin stitch using pale yellow stranded cotton. The feelers, feet and an eye are worked in straight stitch using one thread of black stranded cotton.

Finally sew some bronze bugle beads in the inner curves of the upper two tendrils and some cream pearls around the throat to form a necklace and your embroidery is complete. Block following the directions given on page 14 and then take your embroidery to your picture framer. Next sit back and enjoy the company of your own woodland nymph!

Evening Bag

An evening out is a good excuse for dressing up and this bag is the perfect accompaniment for an elegant evening.

In making this bag I selected just one motif, the honeysuckle, which I then repeated across the front of the bag at different angles. I selected the honeysuckle, as I felt the seed shape lent itself to repetition with the scattering of individual chain stitches and beads within the areas created by the random pintucking, which is also a feature of this bag. The embroidery was stitched using a random dyed thread because I enjoy the subtle colour changes that occur when using these threads.

Trace the pattern for the front flap and gusset on page 99. Now fold the fabric selvage to selvage and cut in half. Refer to the pattern layout on page 101 before cutting out the gusset and *tacking* the outline of the pattern for the front flap. *Do not* cut out the front flap until embroidery is completed. Next transfer the honeysuckle motif outline to the fabric. Personally I prefer to use sewing tracing paper when transferring designs to dark fabrics but use whichever method you find easiest. Don't forget to iron on interlining to strengthen the silk before you start to stitch.

With your ch osen thread chain stitch round the petals, seeds, buds and leaves on the design and fill with detached buttonhole stitch. Pad, all but the seeds, just a little. I sewed a large amber coloured diamante in the centre of each honeysuckle. To highlight the buds and leaves I used bronze metallic thread for the vein markings on the leaves and for the three little straight stitches on the buds. I also sewed bronze beads here and there to add a little 'glitz' to the bag. For detailed instructions on how to stitch the honeysuckle please refer to page 50. Refer to the photograph on page 57 for additional detail. Block if required.

GUSSET PATTERN *add a seam allowance of 1 cm all around*

trim to required length when fitted

finished length 54 cm including seam allowance
finished width 6.5 cm including seam allowances
tapering to 4.5 cm

add 3 cms here

place on fold

FRONT FLAP PATTERN *add a seam allowance of 1 cm all around - finished size 10 x 24.5 cm including seam allowances*

extend here for front and back pattern pieces

placement line for couched cord

solid dots show placement of beads

REQUIREMENTS

(finished size 24.5 x 14 cm)

- 0.5 m fabric 115 cm wide - we used silk
- 0.3 m lining
- threads of your choice - I used a random dyed cotton thread and a bronze metallic thread
- glass beads
- cord hand made or bought
- couching thread
- wadding/needle punch
- magnetic bag clasp or large dome/s

SCALED DOWN PATTERN PIECES

with 1 cm seam allowance added

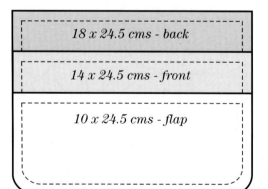

18 x 24.5 cms - back

14 x 24.5 cms - front

10 x 24.5 cms - flap

TO MAKE THE BAG

Trace, then cut out pattern pieces for the bag front 14 x 24.5 cm and the bag back 18 x 24.5 cm, see diagram below. Use the front flap pattern as a guide to give you the correct curve for the rounded end on the other two pattern pieces and extend along the dotted edge.

The second half of the fabric is randomly pintucked as shown by the dotted lines in the pattern layout diagram on page 101. The lines are a guide only. When you have finished your random pintucking iron the fabric face down on to a folded towel. Now place the pattern pieces for the front and back of the bag on the fabric making best use of the pintucked shapes. Mark or tack the outlines.

Choose some of the areas made by the pintucking and fill these with detached chain stitches. Sew some tiny bronze glass beads on with metallic thread inside the detached chain stitches. Place the beads at least 1 cm away from the bag outline so they and your sewing machine will not be damaged when making up the bag. Cut out front, front flap and back pieces of the bag.

Fold the back of the bag (the biggest piece) under 1.5 cm along the straight edge and place the embroidered front flap of the bag under the fold with raw edges together. With the right sides of the fabric facing sew right across the bag 6 mm back from the fold, creating a tuck. This is now the 'main' bag piece.

Cut out needlepunch/wadding the same size as the main and front bag pieces and tack to each piece.

If a magnetic clasp is to be used, it has to be fitted at this point following the manufacturer's instructions.

Cut lining for both bag pieces and place behind the needlepunch. To hold all three layers together (silk, needlepunch and lining) zigzag through all thicknesses around all raw edges.

Cut bias in strips 4.5 cms wide from remaining fabric that *was not* pintucked. With right sides together pin a bias strip across the straight opening edge of the bag front and stitch 1 cm from edge. Do not trim. Fold and turn bias back inside the bag, fold under raw edge and secure by hand.

Cut a gusset lining and baste the gusset and lining together.

Align the centre of the gusset with the centre of the lower edge of the bag front. With wrong sides together pin gusset to the bag front starting at the centre and working around to the opening edge of the bag. You will need to ease the gusset around the corners of the bag. The top of the gusset (it is a little narrower here than at the base) should finish just *below* the bottom edge of bias stitched across the opening edge. Cut gusset to this measurement and bias trim both ends to neaten in the same way as you neatened the opening edge of the bag.

Aligning the centres and with wrong sides together pin the gusset to the main bag piece, once again easing around the corners, then sew both sides of the gusset to the bag using a 1 cm seam allowance.

Bias trim all remaining outer edges.

Couch the cord in position as shown on the front flap pattern, securing couching thread under tuck at upper edge to neaten.

Close with dome/s if not using a magnetic clasp.

Let the elegant evening begin!

PATTERN LAYOUT

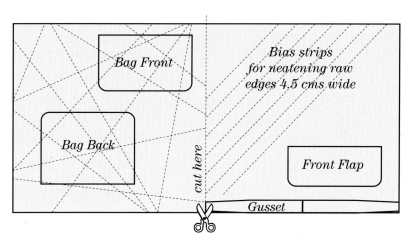

BIBLIOGRAPHY

Synge, L. ed., *The Royal School Book of Needlework and Embroidery.* Wm Collins Sons & Co Ltd, London, 1986.

Swain, M. H., *Historical Needlework A Study of Influences Scotland and Northern England.* Barry & Jenkins, London, 1970.

Snook, B., *English Embroidery.* Mills & Boon, London, 1974.

Warner, P., *Embroidery A History.* Batsford, London, 1991.

Proctor, M., *Needlework Tools and Accessories.* Batsford, London, 1990.

Sebba, A., *Samplers Five Centuries of a Gentle Craft.* Weidenfeld and Nicolson, London, 1979.

Wingfield Digby, G., *Elizabethan Embroidery.* Faber, London, 1963.

Conversion Chart of DMC Threads to Au Ver a Soie Threads

DMC Coton a broder 16 (called Brilliant Cutwork and Emb. Thread in USA)   **Au Ver A Soie Perlee**

DMC Numbers	approximate colour	Perlee Numbers	DMC Numbers	approximate colour	Perlee Numbers
48	variegated pink	767	740	orange	299
101	variegated green	use selection of greens	742	dark yellow	227
211	mauve	348	743	yellow	679
223	Paris pink	494	754	soft pink	134
224	medium Paris pink	177	782	mustard	303
301	rust	525	792	violet blue	768 but use 652 for grapes
336	dark blue	441	793	light violet blue	427
349	red	681 but use 106 for bird	797	royal blue	652
367	medium green	549	799	medim blue	018
369	light green	383	800	light blue	417
469	olive green	491	801	dark brown	205
471	light olive green	734	815	ruby red	109
504	light sea green	058	840	medium brown	517
552	purple	447	904	apple green	491
553	medium purple	190	930	slate blue	313
561	dark mint green	620	945	peach	155
562	mint green	547	973	hard yellow	679
563	light mint green	763	3032	taupe	572
602	raspberry pink	393	3326	pink	176
677	pale old gold	147	3328	coral	633
701	bright green	061	3689	light raspberry pink	076
702	light bright green	394	3782	fawn	538
727	citrus yellow	776	ecru		creme

OTHER PUBLICATIONS

Exploring Embroidery
- five different techniques with ten different projects published in full colour

The Elizabethan Needlework Series
Exploring Elizabethan Embroidery
- the first book in the series - introducing stitches and techniques used in this embroidery with seven different projects to embroider

Elizabethan Needlework Accessories
- the second book in the series - introducing further stitches and techniques with more projects on a needlework theme, to embroider

Festive Elizabethan Creations
- the third book in the series - exquisite Elizabethan embroidery for the special occasions in your life

An Elizabethan Christmas
- beautiful Christmas decorations inspired by the life and times of the Elizabethans

Other Publications
Time for Beads
A fascinating introduction to a variety of hand-held beading projects. Your chance to use some of the beautiful beads which are now available.

From My Hands
Introducing exquisite counted satin stitch and pulled thread designs. Elegant and crisp this embroidery is a joy to see and do!

Forthcoming titles
An Elizabethan Alphabet and Monograms - a beautiful and very personal way to use this embroidery

Olwyn's Exceptional Sampler - a Prizewinning Sampler for you to create.

Plus more exciting titles

Georgeson Publishing Limited
PO Box 100-667, North Shore Mail Centre, New Zealand
Tel: 64 9 410 2079 Fax: 64 9 410 2069
Email: gpl@georgeson.co.nz   Website: www.georgeson.co.nz